LUV×
ESTHER

Nancy Goudie

New Wine Press

New Wine Ministries
PO Box 17
Chichester
West Sussex
United Kingdom
PO20 6YB

Scripture quotations are taken from the following versions of the Bible:

NIV – The Holy Bible, New International Version. Copyright © 1973, 1978, 1984 by International Bible Society. Used by permission of Hodder and Stoughton Limited.

The Message. Copyright © 1993, 1994, 1995, 1996, 2000, 2001, 2002 by Eugene H. Peterson

ISBN 1–903725–60–7

Photography by Dave Pratt and Cat Taylor (CT Images)
Original Luv Esther design by Wilf Witty
Cover design by CCD, www.ccdgroup.co.uk
Typeset by CRB Associates, Reepham, Norfolk
Printed in Malta

Dedication

I want to dedicate this book to two "Esthers" who have made a deep imprint on my life:

- **Heidi Baker** – a missionary in Mozambique whose life story of serving Jesus has so inspired me.

- **Mary McVicar**, my dear Mum, who throughout her life always taught me to "lay down my life for Jesus".

Also to the amazing **Luv Esther cast, crew, production team, project management team** and **partners** especially **John and Rose Lancaster** without whom Luv Esther would not have happened.

Credits

I want to thank the following people for the love and encouragement they have given me through the writing of this book:

- **To my husband and best friend, Ray**. You consistently encourage me throughout life – thank you for all the help you gave in the writing of this book. Without your amazing vision for Luv Esther, this book would not have been possible.

- Thank you to **Murray Watts** who also read the manuscript and gave me such helpful comments and advice.

- Thank you to **Lucy** who has helped me in a practical way by looking after my son, Aidan, when I needed to work and to **Beth**, my personal assistant, and **all at ngm** for your constant encouragement and support.

- To **Tim Pettingale** for your encouragement and your continued belief in me – it's always a joy to work with you.

And most of all, thank you to the "**Unseen Conductor**" who continues to make His presence known. Forever I want to love and serve You.

About the Author

Nancy Goudie, along with her husband, Ray, has been in full-time Christian ministry since 1980 when they left Scotland with a vision from God to start a ministry through which God could reach the youth of their land. In 1981 Ray and Nancy founded and led the internationally known band Heartbeat which later became known as ngm. As one of the singers and main speakers Nancy travelled and ministered throughout the UK and abroad and saw a mighty move of God's Spirit with thousands of people being touched by the power of God and swept into the Kingdom.

Although Heartbeat finished in 1991, Nancy's gifts of preaching and teaching have continued to be used through the ministry of ngm, not only in Britain, but also in mainland Europe and the USA. Her passion and love for Jesus is evident to all who meet her. She has also been interviewed on radio and television numerous times about her faith in God and has a regular radio show called *A Slice of Life* on UCB radio. She also runs a unique creative conference for women each year in a luxury hotel in Bristol.

Nancy has written six books as well as many articles for magazines and newspapers. She has also recorded three powerful meditation CDs through which many have come into a deeper and more intimate walk with Jesus.

Nancy and her husband Ray have two sons, Daniel (18) and Aidan (8).

To find out more about Nancy and the work she does visit her website at www.nancygoudie.com or www.ngm.org.uk

NGM PRESENTS

LUVx
ESTHER

Written by
RAY GOUDIE / MURRAY WATTS

Directed by
MURRAY WATTS

Produced by
RAY GOUDIE

Music Produced by
KEVAN FROST / RAY GOUDIE

Choreography
SUZY MILLS

Set Design
SEAN CAVANAGH

Lighting Design
BEN CRACKNELL

Mix and Digital Production
ALAN BRANCH

Video Director
DAVE NEAL

Contents

Setting the Scene

The excitement is growing; tension fills the air; what is about to happen? What am I going to see? The lights suddenly go out, excitement ripples through the crowd, cheers and applause fill the hall. The haunting music starts, on the video screen a star shines, the video then portrays a young orphan girl walking through the desert; she is a stranger in a strange land. Images of war flash before our eyes, lightning strikes . . . and the musical journey through *Luv Esther* has begun. For many the journey of seeing the performance of *Luv Esther* has just started, however, for Ray and me the journey of *Luv Esther* began a long time before on a beach in the Algarve.

Ray and I were on sabbatical and as well as enjoying the rest and the sun, we were also searching God's heart for the years ahead. We had served Him for twenty years and seen Him do so much, but what did God want for the years that lay ahead? As Ray lay in the sun reading an autobiography by Tim Rice which told the story of musicals such as *Joseph* and *Jesus Christ Superstar* a seed of inspiration dropped into his heart. He leaned over to me and said, "Do you think God could be calling me to write a musical?" It sounded such a huge vision, but as we talked we had no idea just how big a vision it was going to be!

The exciting thing about following Jesus is that you never know where you might end up. He has the knack of putting a little seed in your heart and as you allow Him to water it and be the guardian of your vision, it begins to grow before your eyes and gradually your dream becomes a reality. We have often said that following God is never boring – tiring, yes, but boring never! What a journey God started that day in the summer of 2000 in the Algarve.

As the seed of inspiration began to grow, the story of Esther almost picked itself. The biblical story of Esther is so full of drama, fear, courage and hope. It tells a compelling story which is full of love and beauty, and yet hatred and ugliness are never far away. It's the story of how one seemingly insignificant orphan girl overcame her fear and saved her nation from total destruction. What a story! Tim Rice has said that when you are writing a musical it is essential that you have three things: a good story, a good story, and a good story! For Ray, Esther was *the* story; not just a good story but an extraordinary one!

I believe that the story of Esther resonates with us, the Church, at this time. It is a prophetic voice calling us, the Bride, to deeper intimacy with the King of kings and out of this intimacy to make a difference as we reach out with His love and compassion to the poor. Ray's prayer has always been that *Luv Esther* would be a vehicle to see people fall headlong in love with Jesus and raise up an army of "Esthers" who fulfil their destiny "for such a time as this".

In telling the story of *Luv Esther*, I have intentionally told Ray's and my personal journey. There are a great many people involved in *Luv Esther* from the cast, crew, to the whole production team who all have their own stories to tell. I want to take this opportunity of honouring all involved in *Luv Esther* – their contribution to this production has been invaluable. We have had an amazing journey and gained many wonderful friends. This book uses a lot of our own illustrations and highlights how God has taken a couple of very ordinary people and through God's grace has done some extraordinary things. I hope that our stories and Esther's story encourage you that God can take you and use you in wonderful ways.

In this book, I will not only take you through the scenes from the story of Esther as well as the background scenes to the musical being written, but I will also provide you with notes that will help you to study the book of Esther. I know that as you study this book, you will fall in love with the heroine of the story. Esther is an amazing woman, yet an ordinary person too, with little going for her. She would never have guessed that she would transform the destiny of her nation. This story proves that any of us, even although we feel insignificant can make a huge difference. Interestingly, it is the only book in the Bible where there is no mention of God. Not once does His name appear on its pages and yet God's presence is felt through every page. My prayer is that you will not only enjoy this amazing, intriguing story, but also that you will meet the One who made it all happen, the "Unseen Conductor", as Ray calls Him, and that you would fall headlong in love with Him and realise that He has called you, "for such a time as this".

The Main Characters

King Xerxes ruled the vast Persian Empire from Susa, his capital (where the story of Esther takes place). He had been king for seven years when Esther first stepped onto the scene. Xerxes was the most powerful man on earth at that time (479 BC).

Esther was the beautiful adopted daughter of Mordecai. Her Persian name means "star", a reference to the star-like flowers of myrtle as well as a "star in the sky" and her Jewish name, Hadassah, comes from the word for "myrtle". Myrtle is a lowly shrub, but the word in Hebrew means "fragrance". Both names express Esther's character perfectly. She was an orphan child, a humble Jew living in exile, yet she leaves an exotic fragrance on the pages of history. Esther was a woman of great strength and dignity, "beautiful in form and lovely to look at", but a woman who discovered the secret of spiritual courage and inner beauty.

Mordecai, like Esther, was a descendant of the Jews who had been forced into exile by the fall of Jerusalem about one hundred years before. Many were now living throughout the Persian Empire and surviving in a dangerous and hostile world. Mordecai took his much younger cousin, Esther, an orphan, to be his own daughter and brought her up in the faith. He is an example of great integrity and bravery and is best remembered for his immortal challenge to Esther to risk her life and use her influence as queen to save her people: "Who knows whether you have come to the kingdom for such a time as this."

Haman was the villain of the story. He was deceitful,
conceited, anti-Semitic – the sworn enemy of the Jews.
Haman was a wealthy and influential officer in the court of
the king, who rose to the highest influence in the land. He was
enraged by Mordecai's refusal to pay him respect and this
confrontation fuelled his murderous plan to destroy the entire
Jewish nation. There is classic villainy and even melodrama in
Haman's rise and fall, but the history of the last two thousand
years, above all the horrors of the twentiethth century, show
that his story is grimly prophetic. An absurd figure, obsessed
with his own celebrity and power, he rises to high office with
an evil agenda.

Like all good stories, Esther has subplots and minor
characters, including **Vashti** the first queen, **Bigthan and
Teresh**, eunuchs and royal officials who plot an assassination
attempt on Xerxes, **Zeresh**, Haman's wife who persuades him
to build a huge gallows for Mordecai, and the chief eunuch in
charge of the women, **Hegai**. It is Hegai who spots Esther's
royal potential.

ACT ONE

Prologue

Many years ago in a land far, far away began an amazing story full of intrigue, drama, beauty, glamour, hatred, pride and greed. As the haunting sounds of the Prologue invade the air, the story opens on stage with the picture of a beautiful, innocent, Jewish, orphan girl walking through the desert. She is a refugee – a product of war. We see images of newspapers which give glimpses of the story ahead. We also see pictures of Mordecai (Esther's surrogate dad) who looked after her as she grew up in this strange and often cruel world. As you read the biblical story of Esther, it is obvious even from the beginning that Esther and Mordecai had a special relationship that was overflowing with a fatherly love.

The story of Esther is set, not in Palestine, nor even Babylon, but farther east in the capital of the vast Persian empire. In 597 BC King Nebuchadnezzar invaded the land of Judah, deported the king to Babylon and removed the treasures from the temple. Eleven years later he returned and then destroyed Jerusalem and took most of the Jews into captivity. In 539 BC Babylon itself was invaded and was defeated by the Medes and the Persians. Xerxes (or Ahasuerus, his Hebrew name) became King in 486 BC. Xerxes therefore ruled the biggest and most powerful nation in the known world at that time. The book of Esther happens while most of the Jews are still living in exile and is marked by the fact that even in exile, God had not forgotten His people.

Esther's Persian name means "star", but her Jewish name "Hadassah" means "myrtle" which in Hebrew means "fragrance". Both names are so significant and appropriate, for it is obvious from the beginning that she is the "star" of the show. Her beauty and the loveliness of her character shine brightly for all to see, but she also has a "fragrance" which drips onto every page of her story. It says in the Bible that Esther was lovely in form and features (Esther 2:7). In other words, she was lovely both inside and out. This is obvious from the moment you see her fresh, innocent face on the screen.

Can you imagine what it must have been like for this young, fragile girl to have grown up in a foreign land, an orphan and a refugee with no rights or nationality? We are told in Esther 2:7 that Esther had neither father nor mother, but fortunately for her, she had a cousin called Mordecai who was a kind and godly man who adopted her as his own daughter. He taught her well and she loved and respected him for all he had sacrificially given to her as we will see in later chapters.

As the haunting music of the Prologue concludes, what is not said in the musical *Luv Esther* is that Xerxes, who was the most powerful ruler on earth, had just had a banquet to display his vast wealth.

They certainly knew how to party in those days for this celebration lasted 180 days, or put another way, six months! (Esther 1:4). After that was finished, it's clear he wasn't tired of partying because he had another banquet. This one lasted just seven days – quite short by his standards – but it was at the end of this banquet when he and his guests had probably had too much to drink that he wanted to parade his wife's beauty for all to see. He gives the command for his wife to come to his side, but Esther 1:12 tells us that Vashti, his wife, refuses to obey the most powerful man in the world, thus releasing his wrath upon her. We don't know exactly what happened to Queen Vashti after that, but she was banished from his presence, never to see the face of the King again. It is possible that her life was terminated as Xerxes was a proud King who lived in cruel times. Neither do we know why she refused to obey the King, but we do know that her position as Queen was to be given to someone else.

Biblical scholars tell us that a number of years then went by where it is likely that Xerxes was very busy in a war with Greece. It is after this time that he began to miss his beautiful wife. His royal advisors advised him to look for a replacement that would be even more beautiful than Vashti. Suddenly, the news was released – the King is looking for a beautiful bride!

Chapter 1

Everybody's Talking

Have you heard the news? Who do you think it will be? Could it be me? Could it be you? A buzz of excitement went through the air ... the gossip columns were full of the details ... the citadel of Susa was alive with the news: the King was looking for a Queen.

As the first notes of the opening song, "Everybody's Talking", penetrate the senses of the audience, suddenly the stage is full of excitement and colour. As the song starts, the cast dressed in amazing outfits, sing and dance the news across the specially designed stage (see page 28). The King had issued a command and many girls' lives were about to change. As Ray points out in this song, if this had happened in our day, then *OK* and *Hello*, the glam magazines, would have had all the gossip on its front pages. The televisions would have been full of the dramatic news that the King was going to choose hundreds of girls throughout his land to come to live in the Palace and be pampered with beauty treatments and that one special girl would be chosen to be his Queen.

It's got everybody talking
TV ratings soar
Photos in OK, Hello
Who will pay for more?
Auditions held in every town
Walk on through the door
The polls are showing who's in front
You feel the tension grow.

Searching for a star
To make somebody's dream
So many girls, so many dreams
Of joining the royal scene
Looking for the one
Summoned by command
Can such a one for such a time
Be found throughout the land?

Who will wear the bridal dress?
Is anybody's guess
Beauty treatments are on tap
Trying to impress
The Palace is the place to be
Blondes, redheads, brunettes,
Competition is intense
It's time to place your bets.

Written by Ray Goudie/Mark Vallance
Published by Curious? Music UK/ngm/MCA Music Ltd © 2005

Although they did not have a media world like ours, it
would not have been long before everyone in Xerxes' vast
kingdom had heard the news. The King was looking for a
Queen and it could be any one of thousands of young virgin
girls throughout the land. What a story! What a scoop! The
talk of Xerxes' vast nation would be: who was going to be
chosen as the new Queen?

Bible Study Notes

Read Esther 1 – 2:4

1. Look up the word "chosen" in the dictionary and write down its meaning.

2. 1 Peter 2:9 tells us we are a chosen people. Each one of us is chosen by God. Discuss or think through how this makes you feel. Meditate on this verse and write down/ discuss what God says through it.

3. Romans 5:8 tells us that God loved us and died for us while we were still far away from Him. His love for us is amazing. Isaiah 46:3–4 tells us that God cares for us and loves us throughout the whole of our lives. Dwell on this (if in a group, discuss this) and write down how you feel knowing that God's hand has been on you throughout the whole of your life.

4. We sometimes find words like **special, chosen, beautiful**, difficult to accept about ourselves. Think through/ discuss why this should be and take your answers to God. It may be you should discuss your answers with a pastor/ mentor or someone you respect in God.

The cast rehearsing on Sean Cavanagh's amazing stage set

The stage set was designed by Sean Cavanagh who has been responsible
for creating the sets for *Joseph and His Technicolour Dreamcoat* and
The Rat Pack shows in the West End of London. Murray Watts arranged a
meeting between Ray and Sean and when he heard what we were doing
he agreed to design the set for *Luv Esther*. It was one of these meetings
organised and arranged by the "Unseen Conductor". Sean has done an
amazing job – the set he designed is just so perfect for the story of
Luv Esther.

Chapter 2

Ordinary day/I wonder

It was just another ordinary day
Oh yeah, oh yeah
Talking on the phone nothing to say
Oh yeah, oh yeah
Ordinary
Ordinary day

It hit me with such force no warning shot
Right between the eyes
I'm reeling from the shock
Woke up this morning
I got a call to win a dream
The prize a king-sized bed.

Written by Ray Goudie/Kevan Frost
Published by Curious? Music UK/ngm/MCS Music Ltd © 2005

It was just another ordinary day in the citadel of Susa, nothing to mark it out as being different, but this day was going to change the lives of many of the young, beautiful girls who lived in those dark and grey times. To these girls it was just an ordinary day, but it was a day which would change their lives dramatically.

When Ray was writing *Luv Esther* he likened this part of the show to a beauty contest. Many beautiful girls were being taken from their homes, but only one was going to be chosen. Hundreds of girls were plucked from obscurity into the limelight of the Palace, but only one of them was going to win the prize! What was the prize? As Ray wrote, tongue in cheek – a King-sized bed! One of them was going to end up being married to the King.

Can you imagine what it would have been like for all these girls? They were taken from their homes and told from now on they would live at the Palace. On the face of it, it would seem to be an amazing journey. They would be pampered with beauty treatments for a year; fed with the best food and wine; given beautiful robes to wear; educated in etiquette to match the surroundings of the King; being able to have whatever they wanted until they were ready to go and spend the night in the King's royal residence. It may have seemed like bliss and no doubt some of it was, however on the down side, they would never again live with the families that they loved. They would know that only one of them would win the prize of being made Queen. If they were rejected they would have to live in another part of the harem, banished forever, never to be summoned again. If that happened to them then whatever dreams they had of falling in love, getting married or having children were gone forever. What a trauma for these young virgin girls to go through, to say nothing of the fact that they would have to sleep with a man who they had only seen from afar, who was probably double their age and who would not think twice about ending their lives if he felt like it. These were indeed cruel times.

No doubt because of Esther's natural beauty and also, I believe, because of God's plan, Esther was one of the girls chosen to be pampered by beauty treatments before being ushered into the King's bedroom. She had no choice. She had to go; but before she left the only home and the only parent she had ever known, Mordecai, instructed her not to mention the fact that she was a Jew.

As Esther was taken away, I am sure many questions and fears would have filled her mind. What is going to happen to me? How am I going to survive without my "dad" and my friends? Will I ever see them again? Where are you God? Are you listening? Do you see what is happening to me? So many unanswered questions! Have you ever felt like that? Something happens to you and suddenly your world has changed. Fear and anxiety fills your mind – you don't understand what is going on. Your cry goes up, "God where are You? Do You see what is happening to me? Can You hear me God? Why are You not answering me?" Have you ever felt like that? Have you ever asked God these questions?

I certainly have and so have many millions of other people at different times down the centuries. The Psalms are full of David asking God these kinds of questions. It is not wrong to ask questions; however it is good to ask with the knowledge that no matter what happens, God is with you throughout whatever storm you are going through. In Luke 8 we read about a furious storm which happened when Jesus and His disciples were in a boat crossing the lake of Galilee. The disciples would have been experienced sailors as many of them had been fishermen, so the storm must have been very bad. They looked around for Jesus, but He was fast asleep. They woke Him up with their cries, "Jesus, don't You care? Wake up Jesus, we are going to drown." Jesus simply said to them, "Where is your faith?" In other words, "Don't you realise that with Me in the boat you are safe? Could you not just trust Me?"

Do you know that Jesus is with you no matter how bad the storms of life become? He will never leave you nor forsake you. His voice echoes down throughout the centuries, "Will you trust Me to work everything out for you?"

Mordecai Makes His Entrance

As the dancers fade away into the dark recesses of the stage, Mordecai makes his entrance and takes centre stage. As he sings the song "I wonder" the lyrics begin to tell us the different emotions that he is struggling with. The Bible tells us that Mordecai had looked after Esther as if she were his own daughter. Now he would no longer be able to take care of her. She would have to "fly" by herself. This excerpt from the song "I wonder" exposes his love, his concerns and his fears.

How the years have gone fast
Memories of your storied past
Orphan child, special gift of love
How I've loved you so,
I have to let you go.

You have been a daughter to me
Walked right into my family
Oh the tears I have prayed for you
Make your path on the earth, and show
Your heart is whiter than the snow.

I wonder, I wonder,
What does this mean?
Yeah, what does this all mean?
I wonder, I wonder,
Is this a royal dream?

Written by: Ray Goudie/Neil Wilson
Published by Curious? Music UK/ngm © 2005

You can hear the confusion in his mind. What will happen to Esther? I can't protect her any longer. She has to go and I have to let her go! But maybe, just maybe God, You are in this! I wonder? I wonder? Is this in Your plan? Have You engineered this Lord? Is this Your will for her life? I have to give her over to You Lord. I have to let her go.

Esther and Mordecai had no idea that Esther was at the beginning of an amazing journey which would take her into the heart of the King. Both their lives would be completely and utterly changed and through their faith and trust in God they would literally "save" a nation. God was certainly with them and in all that was happening.

In 2003, God spoke to Ray and me and told us He wanted us to come up close to Him as there was something He wanted to say. Like Esther and Mordecai, we knew we were at the beginning of a journey but we had no idea where that journey would take us. We had no idea that it would literally change the face of ngm (the missionary work we founded in the early 80s); that most of us would be completely different people; that God would prune us and through the pain of pruning make us more fruitful. Looking back, it is a journey that we would not have wanted to miss and had we known that as well as joy, fun, laughter, we would also experience pain, sorrow, heartache and suffering we would still have jumped into it with open arms.

Esther must have felt the same. Emotions like fear, loneliness, hopelessness must have dominated her thoughts and yet somewhere in the back of her mind, I am sure she would have told God that she trusted Him and said as Jesus did many years later, "Not my will, Lord, but Yours be done."

When we encounter situations that seem very difficult, it is comforting to remember God's word to us through the prophet, Jeremiah: "For I know the plans I have for you, declares the Lord, plans to prosper you and not to harm you, plans to give you a hope and a future." God has our best interests at heart. No matter what you are going through, always remember that God is in control. Nothing takes Him by surprise and through every pathway God is weaving His divine will for your life.

Bible Study Notes

Read Esther 2:5–11

1. Esther grew up with no Mum or Dad. Mordecai, her cousin was her only parent figure. Write down some of the issues that Esther may have had to face because this was the case.

2. Verse 10 says that Esther did not reveal her nationality because Mordecai had "forbidden" her to do so. See verse 20 for further information. What does this say about Esther's character and her relationship with Mordecai? How can we learn from this? How can we develop a teachable spirit?

3. Verse 11 says that Mordecai walked back and forth near the courtyard of the harem to find out how Esther was and what was happening to her. What does this say about Mordecai? How can we learn from this?

4. When Esther was taken away from Mordecai and began to live in the Palace, write down some of the emotions she may have been feeling as she was taken away from the only "dad" she knew.

I'm sure Esther did not understand what was happening to her and she must have wondered what God was doing. Discuss/think through similar situations that have happened in your own life and write down what you can learn through the story of Esther.

Chapter 3

Everybody's Looking for Love

From the moment that Hegai appears on stage his presence fills the stage. He is a very colourful, engaging character who you just can't help but love. Hegai is the chief eunuch who is put in charge of these beautiful young virgins and as the song says – who wouldn't like that job?

I've gotta difficult task, I wanna ask
Can you do it or would you blow it?
I say find that one show them to the king
I got a girl who's got everything, everything
Say you know what I have a difficult job
I gotta whole lot of women all day gotta listen to
Gotta look gotta feel, gotta know what's real
You know what I mean
I be checking out the lookers, don't want hookers,
Lazy lovers, I don't want losers
I want a girl with the shine
Fit for the king that's right
She gotta have style
I'm an expert flirt when it comes to the skirt
I'm famous, I got clout, I'm a talent scout
It's hard but I gotta keep real coz

Everybody's looking for love in their life
Everybody's looking for love
Everybody's looking for love in their life
Everybody's looking for love

Hegai has been given the "difficult" task of looking after 400 beautiful women and Esther very quickly catches his eye. He sees that she is not only beautiful to the eye but her inner life is beautiful too.

Saw this girl shining like a star in the sky
No doubt this girl was like heaven sent
Stepped out from the crowd like a ray in the cloud
Sunlight be pouring, rivals adoring
Set the whole harem up on fire
She was hot hot hot like fire
Man oh man taking me higher
Night disappearing, the dawn was bright
Got goose bumps at my very first sight
When she moved it was like mystery
From the world beyond changing history
Believe me I ain't got it wrong
She was song without singing
She knocked me out
She had that sweet look differential
Esther had that royal potential

Written by Murray Watts/Kevan Frost/George Mhondera/Ray Goudie
Published by Copyright control/MCS Music Ltd/Curious? Music Uk/
ngm © 2005

In a world so foreign to her, Esther immediately stands out from the crowd. We, too, live in a world which is so different from the Kingdom of Heaven, the question each of us needs to ask ourselves is – do we stand out from the crowd? Is it obvious that we are different from the citizens of this world? Not necessarily because of what we wear but because of what we say, do and act. The world we live in is so full of greed, selfishness and pride. Are we always looking after number one? The adverts tell us, "If it feels good do it," in other words, don't worry about anyone else but you.

I'm sure some of you will have received letters from banks and credit cards offering loans which many people cannot repay. We received one from our own bank which said, "Why wait, when you can have it all now?" The message from the world is designed to feed selfishness and greed. I believe as Christians, we are called to be different.

We live in a society that is surprised when people tell the truth. The society we live in often expects people to tell untruths or at best twist the truth to suit our own needs. I recently told a hotel that they had missed off some charges on my bill. Their response was to tell me that they thought I was stupid to have brought it to their attention! When we live God's way, we will certainly stand out as being different – Esther immediately stood out. On stage when the girls appear in their glitzy costumes which emphasise the type of girl they are, it is so obvious that Esther is different, not only by what she wears, but by how she acts. Her innocence and purity makes sure that Hegai spots her potential and immediately moves her to the best part of the harem (Esther 2:9). It is here that she begins her beauty treatments.

Bible Study Notes

Read Esther 2:8–9

1. Esther stood out from the crowd. Discuss/write down the reasons why. How can we stand out from the crowd in today's society and make a difference for God?

2. Esther had the favour of God on her. This part of the story reminds me of Joseph when he was in prison in

Egypt. Even in difficult and awful circumstances, Joseph found favour with the prison warden (Genesis 39:22). Write down/discuss what this tells you about our amazing God? Write down what we should remember when we are put into difficult circumstances.

3. Esther was beautiful on the outside but she was also beautiful on the inside. At the height of the "beauty contest" especially, she would have been surrounded by greedy, selfish and worldly women, yet she was seen to be different. Discuss/write down what made Esther beautiful on the inside and what we can learn from this.

Chapter 4

Breathe on Me

Facials, manicures, pedicures, full body massages and body wraps – the Palace is now the best health and beauty resort in the known world!

The mood in the show changes as Esther and her handmaidens begin the process of drenching Esther in the fragrance of the Palace. This is the bit that all women everywhere would love. Just imagine what it would have been like. A whole *year* of beauty treatments, facials, massages, pedicures and manicures. Wow! Doesn't that sound fantastic? The Palace was fast becoming the best health and beauty resort known at that time. What these treatments did was to remove the aroma of the "outside world" from each girl. Esther had six months with the oil of myrrh and six months with perfumes and cosmetics. These treatments would have been designed to remove all toxins from the body as well as cleansing and purifying the skin. The regular bathing and application of myrrh would soften and tone the skin. The six months of perfumes and cosmetics would saturate the skin until Esther literally spread fragrance throughout the palace wherever she would go. Oh, how we need to have the "outside world" removed from us and to be so drenched in Jesus that wherever we go we take the fragrance of Heaven with us. The song that Esther sings, "Breathe on Me", is like a prayer for God to come and drench her with His love. This is what God wants to do in each of us.

> Breath of life
> Breathe on me
> Let the fire of love touch me
> Breath of life
> Breathe on me
> Let the fire of love touch me.
>
> Written by Ray Goudie/Kevan Frost
> Published by Curious? Music UK/ngm/MCS Music Ltd 2005

Life had changed for Esther. You can imagine if you had spent a year at a health spa just how different you would be. Esther's life was so different; the fragrance of the old life had gone and a new way of life had begun. In many ways what happened to Esther is very similar to what happened to us in 2003. We weren't drenched in oils and perfumes, but we were drenched in God's presence and love. We fell in love with Him all over again and our cry became, "God, I want less of me and more of You. I want to be like You. No matter where I go, I want people to smell You from me. I don't want them to smell pride, selfishness, jealousy or any other sin that so easily tangles itself up in our lives, but I want them to experience the fragrance of Jesus." What happened was amazing. I can only describe what happened to us in 2003 as a "move of God" that has changed the face of ngm. In many ways it feels like an "Esther anointing" where the Bride of Christ is being prepared for the Bridegroom.

As I said earlier it all started with us hearing God say some simple words, "Come up close, there are things I want to say to you." In response to that Ray started getting up very early in the morning to seek God. The first thing God said to him was, "Ray, you are My beloved son," and those words wrecked him with the love of God. A couple of weeks later we went on holiday to the island of Minorca. Each morning, I began to get up early in the morning before everyone else was awake to spend a couple of hours with God by the pool. These times were so special. Later as I met the rest of our household for breakfast, I kept saying that the two hours I spent with God was just not long enough. Ray and I fell in love with Jesus all over again and we just could not get enough of Him. When we came home the hunger in our hearts for more of His presence meant that we continued to get up very early each day. Life changed in the Goudie household. It wasn't "business as usual"; we desperately wanted more of God.

Upon our return from holiday, we shared with the leaders in ngm what God had been doing with us and how we'd been crying out to God for more of Him and much less of us. God met with us and we all ended up on our knees crying out for God to do something in our lives. Ray and I then shared what God had been doing with all the ngm team. What happened was like scenes from some of the revivals I have read about and longed for. Each night as we worshipped, God broke out among us and what happened really surprised us. When we finished preaching, we left a microphone at the front in case people wanted to come and pray or say what God was doing with them. That night and each night since, streams of people came to the front, some to express their hunger for God, some to openly repent of "hidden secrets" in their hearts, while others told God of their longing for revival. We have never witnessed such hunger for God, open confession and repentance like this before. Sins of pride, jealousy, pornography, selfishness, lust and many other deep sins were being openly confessed. I mention more of this in chapter 7. We were and still are being drenched in His fragrance as His presence continues to fall. It is so wonderful. Here's an except from our 2003 newsletter:

> *Each one of us is spending more and more time in the secret place with Jesus early in the morning and as we do our hunger for Him seems to increase like never before. As Ray and I lead the meetings, we often just do not know what to do. We are not in control any more. God is and often we just watch as He moves in the meetings. Ray and I often look at one another and say "What do your think we should do?" and often our answer is "I don't know" and then we laugh because we realise once more that God is doing something really special. We have only had four days of this and already ngm has changed immensely. We cannot even begin to imagine what ngm will look like by the end of October. It's all about Him. Our cries of hunger for Him are disturbing Heaven and He is coming and bringing His presence. Our cry is "Jesus, we want to see Your face; we have to see Your eyes. Please wreck us with Your love." God is calling us to Himself and we are desperate for Him. God is so wonderful.*

And more from our October newsletter:

> *God has been moving in such deep ways – it has been such a privilege to see what we have been seeing. Night after night, God's presence has come in such a way that we are flat on our faces before Him. Many have been confessing deep sins and we have been seeing God deal with issues in minutes that normally would have taken years of counselling to see such a break-through. There is a very deep hunger in our lives for more. The more hunger there is – the more we cry out for Him. God comes and meets us and it fuels our hunger for more. Jesus means everything to us – He means more than life itself. There is a stripping away of ourselves, the killing of our selfish desires and our self life. This has been quite painful in many ways and yet we long to be dead to self.*

Do you want God to breathe the fire of His love on you? Will you allow the fragrance of Jesus to permeate you? Will you be drenched in His Spirit and be ready for an encounter with the King. Esther allowed the fragrance of the Palace oils to become her fragrance and then she was ready to have an encounter with the King.

Bible Study Notes

Read Esther 2:12–14

1. Esther allowed her attendants to bathe her with the fragrant oils etc. How do we allow God to drench us with His love and what would stop you from being drenched in His love? Write down/discuss your answers.

2. When God began to move with us a few years ago the first thing He said was that He loved us. Do you know that God loves you and lavishes His love on you? Meditate on 1 John 3:1a, and ask God to speak to you about this love and write down/discuss what He says.

3. Think through or discuss your relationship with Jesus. Are you living with legalism or is your relationship based on your love relationship with Him? Have you got a hunger for God? What can you do to increase your hunger for Him?

4. When Jesus breathed on His disciples He invited them to receive the Holy Spirit (John 20:22). Spend time praying, asking God to breathe His Holy Spirit upon you. Let yourself be soaked in Him.

Chapter 5

One from Two

Their eyes meet ... the air is charged with passion ... the King has found his Queen ...

This is the wonderful part in the show where the King and Esther meet for the first time and fall in love. Girls, you will particularly love this bit. It is your classic love story. After all the pampering and all the advice is given on what to wear, Esther walks into the royal residence to meet the King. I can just see it in my imagination. The King turns around to see the next young virgin girl who is ready to present herself to him and suddenly their eyes meet and from then on he has eyes for no other. On stage, they begin to dance together. Their eyes are filled with love and the air is charged with passion. The King has made his choice; it's Esther he wants as his Queen. From the minute the King saw Esther he fell headlong in love with her. He couldn't believe what he was seeing, not only was Esther incredibly beautiful but there was something about her that made him say, "Wow!"

**You're beautiful from head to toe, my dear love,
beautiful beyond compare,
Absolutely flawless.** (Song of Songs 4:7, *The Message*)

The words above could have been spoken by Xerxes about Esther, but they weren't, they are written in the most exotic book in the Bible, The Song of Songs. As most commentators will tell you, The Song of Songs is a reflection of how God sees you and me (the Church). Did you know that God has fallen headlong in love with you? Did you know that He looks at you and says "Wow! You are beautiful beyond compare." God sees us as "absolutely flawless" because of all Jesus has done for us on the cross! All our sin and shame are gone forever. He removed them from His sight. He only sees our beauty. We are guilt free! Hallelujah! What wonderful news!

It takes your breath away when you see Esther walking out on stage in her beautiful white wedding dress. This pure and stunningly beautiful girl is willingly giving herself to the King. They begin to sing a beautiful love song to one another called, "One from Two". Esther sings "I'm yours, Majesty" and the King sings back "Let me look on your beautiful, beautiful face." As the words of the song are sung, you almost feel as though you are intruding on a private love scene. It is such an amazing reflection of the King of kings' love for us, His wonderful beautiful Bride.

You've stolen my heart
With one glance of your eyes
Awakened my love
You've aroused my desires
You've lifted up grace
Let me feel your embrace
Arise let me look on your beautiful, beautiful face

Written by Ray Goudie/Mark Underdown
Published by Curious? Music uk/ngm © 2005

Let me ask you again, do you know the Lord loves you? He abundantly and overwhelmingly loves you. As I mentioned before, the first thing God said to us when He asked us to come up close to Him was to tell us that He loved us. It was as if He woke us up with His kiss of love. We didn't know we were asleep, but we were! We were going for God, a team of missionaries on fire for Jesus, and yet we were missing so much of the deeper life. What happened was that we fell headlong in love with Jesus. We've been smitten and we long for more of Him. As the song says, He has stolen our hearts with a glance of His eyes. He's poured out His love on us and everything else has been laid aside. We've fallen in love and we just cannot get enough of Him. He is beautiful, so beautiful. Look into the eyes of Jesus and see the love He has for you. One look, one real look, and you will be over-whelmed forever. You will not be able to miss the love He has for you. Jesus is so wonderful.

One of our team got talking to a girl who worked in a nearby supermarket and invited her to come to one of our ngm Sundays. Later, when she was talking to me, she expressed what it was like walking through the gate into the gardens of Caedmon and into ngm. She told me, "It's like walking into Narnia. You walk through the gate and it's like walking into a completely different world that you didn't know existed." Shortly after that she joined ngm and very quickly fell in love with Jesus. We so need people to "smell" Jesus from us and encounter a different world that they never knew existed. Many people don't recognise a world full of love, compassion and grace because they have hardly experi-enced it. Their world is often filled with darkness, fear, terror and rejection.

Bible Study Notes

Read Esther 2:15–18

1. You will read above that God sees us as "absolutely flawless" because of what Jesus has done for us on the cross. Meditate on Colossians 2:13–15 and write down or discuss what you receive through this. Spend time thanking God for forgiving us.

2. Esther sings in the musical, "I'm yours, Majesty." Write a prayer to God letting Him know that you belong to Him. If you know you do not belong to Jesus, then write down why this is the case and ask Jesus to make Himself known to you.

3. Read Song of Songs 1:2 and spend some time asking God to wake you up and kiss you with His love.

Chapter 6

Welcome to Our World

We're climbing to the top
And you'll never make us stop
Up the greasy pole
Until we find our starring role
We just worship success
No more and no less – Success, success, success
So what if we make an unfortunate mess
Tomorrow our picture will be in the press!

Welcome to our world
It's dingy and it's dark
It's small and tight and filled with night
There's only room for Number one
So fetch a knife or bring a gun
Prepare to fight!

Written by Murray Watts/Kevan frost
Published by Copyright Control/© MCS Music Ltd © 2005

The party is over, the wedding has happened, and the marriage begins. As the fun and celebrations begin to die down, the chief eunuch, Hegai appears on stage to let us know about a small and yet significant situation that happened during those days.

Welcome to the world of Bigthan and Teresh – a world of greed, selfishness and ambition; a world we are not unfamiliar with even thousands of years later. Bigthan and Teresh, two of the King's officers are portrayed on stage by two of our dancers, both of whom are wearing cat suits and masks to give the impression of evil and secrecy, who for some unknown reason became angry with the King and were plotting to assassinate him. These two officers guarded the gate that Mordecai visited each day to see if he could find out any little scrap of information about his beloved "daughter", Esther. What a loving "father" he was. It says in Esther 2:11 that each day he walked back and forth near the courtyard of the harem to find out how Esther was and what was happening to her. One day, as he sat at the King's gate, he *happened* to overhear the conspiracy between Bigthan and Teresh and found a way of getting the news through to Queen Esther. When Esther heard, she reported it to the King, giving the credit to Mordecai. When the King investigated the situation and found it to be true, the two officials were hanged and an account was written in the King's annals.

This seems an insignificant event that is dealt with very quickly but as you read the story you cannot help but wonder why this event is mentioned. However, as the story unfolds you will begin to see that God has been working behind the scenes right from the beginning. It's another one of these times when the "Unseen Conductor" is bringing all the pieces together as we will see in the next few chapters.

Throughout our journey of *Luv Esther*, we have seen the "Unseen Conductor" working behind the scenes again and again. When we first dreamt about *Luv Esther* we had no money for the project and no prospect of raising the finances other than God doing a miracle. At the beginning, whilst Ray and I were praying about this huge venture, Ray was asked by

our dear friends, John and Rose Lancaster, to go on a trip with
them to visit some of the poor areas of South Africa. One day,
whilst relaxing in his hotel, he began to pray about the abject
poverty and the awful situations he had encountered in many
of the places he had visited and pondered on what he/ngm
could do to help. Ray turned to Rose and said, "Do you think
that *Luv Esther* could carry a heart for the poor and needy? Do
you think we could use the vehicle of *Luv Esther* to get the
message out and make people more aware of what is
happening in Africa and elsewhere?" Rose immediately
replied, "Ray, I was just about to say the same to you and if
you do, John and I will definitely help to fund it." John and
Rose Lancaster have given so much to ngm to help us with
the work we do and here they were again being prompted by
the voice of God to stand with us on a major project. Who
would have thought that on a trip to South Africa, God would
provide the bulk of the money for the project as well as give
us an important ingredient for the end of the show? The
"Unseen Conductor" was beginning to bring all the pieces
into play.

Bible Study Notes

Read Esther 2:21–23

1. Mordecai did the right thing by passing on the information he heard as he sat at the gate. He could so easily
   have kept this information to himself. Write down any
   situation in your past where you have found yourself in a
   similar situation. Discuss/think through what you did
   and if you made the right choice?

2. It says in verse 22 that Esther gives credit to Mordecai for
   the news about the planned assassination. This is very
   significant. If she had kept the "glory" for herself and not

mentioned Mordecai, then the outcome could have been very different. She did not allow pride to get in the way, instead her actions showed her pure heart. What can we learn from this?

3. Memorise Psalm 50:10: "Create in me a pure heart, O God, and renew a steadfast spirit within me."

Chapter 7

Don't You Know Who I Am?

Don't you know who I am (Haman, Haman)
Don't you know who I am?
I'm the number one man, superstar
Show me some respect, I don't care who you are.

Don't you know who I am (Haman, Haman)
Don't you know who I am?
I just love the applause, love the fame
Give me some respect come on shout out my name.

Written by Ray Goudie/Neil Wilson
Published by Curious? Music UK/ngm 2005

Enter Haman – the despicable Haman...

One of the most distinctive, powerful characters of the show is Haman – the despicable Haman. He bursts onto the stage looking like a famous rock star wearing a black leather cat suit and face paints and is surrounded by his evil demon dancers. His powerful and catchy song captivates you but you are soon aware that Haman is the villain of the show. He is a proud, wealthy, deceitful character who has an unbelievable hatred for the Jews. He is also a very ambitious man who has reached the heights of his career by becoming the King's right-hand man and yet he still wants more authority and more respect. He is enraged by the fact that Mordecai refuses to bow down to him or pay him respect. Isn't he due this respect? Hasn't the King ordered everyone to honour Haman? Yet, day after day Mordecai refused to obey. When Haman realises that Mordecai is a Jew, he looks for a way to destroy all Jews throughout the whole Kingdom of Xerxes (Esther 3:6). He isn't satisfied with killing one man – he wanted to kill the whole nation of Israel.

It is interesting to note that if you look at Haman's ancestors you will discover that he came from a nation who for generations had hated the Jews. He had allowed his pride and ego to open the door to an intense hatred and evil that had walked through the door of his heart. God said to Cain in Genesis 4:7, "Evil crouches at your door; it desires to have you . . . " It is so easy to open the door of our hearts to evil and allow sin to walk right in. It usually starts with a thought or a desire that we do not throw out but we "play" with in our minds and before we know it, it has taken up residency in our hearts.

In 2005, Ray and I, our two sons and some close friends from ngm, went on holiday to Thailand. We had a wonderful time and stayed in a superb hotel, but as we walked through the streets of Pataya, the nearby town, we were shocked to discover that it was like Soho on heat. Evil seemed to hang in the air. Almost every second shop was a place where young women and young boys were selling their bodies for cash to businessmen. As we walked past, the prostitutes and the drug sellers tried to sell us their wares. We chose to leave but many stayed and sampled the "goods" they had on display. If ever a place needed the love of God that was it. Yet what we saw was probably only the tip of the iceberg. It was a place where evil was being allowed to grow and develop.

It is so easy to register our shock at what we saw, yet the truth is that evil is not far from each of us. Evil lurks around every door, town and city to see who will succumb to its horrific ways. We may never sample the goods of a local prostitute, but pride, selfishness, jealousy, greed, unkind words, anger can be seen in all of us from time to time. The wonderful thing is that as we turn to God He can remove our sins and change our hearts.

When Ray and I brought the message of intimacy to ngm in the autumn of 2003 and shared how we had fallen more deeply in love with Jesus, what happened surprised us. After we preached, we felt we should leave a microphone at the front should people want to come and pray. Streams of people came to the microphone, some to speak out their love and passion for God and some to confess deep hidden sins. Sins such as selfishness, pride, jealousy, anger, as well as lust and pornography were being openly confessed. Ray and I did not preach repentance yet when we spoke of a God who loved us and when His presence fell, all of us realised that before a perfect God, we had all fallen short. We are all sinners saved by grace. Many came to the microphone weeping and asking God to forgive them. The floor of our Caedmon building was literally wet from the tears of those who wept before God. There were many puddles of tears on the floor. People did not want to have hidden sins any longer and could not wait to get rid of the things that had become so entangled around their hearts. Our eyes had been opened and it was so wonderful to see people being set free. Here's an extract from our news-letter in September 2003:

> *Each night as we have worshipped, God has broken out among us. We have wept in repentance before Him. At times people have cried so much that the floor of Caedmon has been wet with the tears of the people crying out to God. We have told people that there is an open microphone at the front if they*

*wish to pray, bring a word, sing or speak out their praises etc.
Each night streams of people are coming to the front, some to
express their hunger for God, some to openly repent of
"secrets" in their hearts while others tell God of their longing
for revival. We have never witnessed open confession and
repentance like this before. Sins of pride, jealousy, pornography, selfishness, lust and many other deep sins are being
openly confessed. God is breaking us and changing lives and
destinies as His presence falls. It is so wonderful. Each one of
us is spending more and more time in the secret place with
Jesus early in the morning and as we do our hunger for Him
seems to increase like never before.*

People were being set free in an instant when it would
normally take months of counselling. It was and is so
wonderful.

As we took the story of what God was doing to people and
churches outside of ngm, we discovered many have "hidden"
secrets in their hearts. Some of those with secrets are people in
church leadership or people who have been Christians for
many years, yet somehow had allowed a "thought" to
germinate in their heart and mind and before long this had
become a major problem. Often because of their position in
leadership, they feel they cannot share their "secret" with
others, and therefore just try and deal with it themselves. This
often leads to a life of double standards. Evil can so easily get
us in its grip and we need the power of God to release us.

If you know you have a secret in your heart that needs to be
dealt with, then my advice would be to share it with someone
you can trust. Ask them to pray for you and get rid of evil's
nasty grip on your heart and life. Our God is wonderful.
When we come back to Him in repentance He responds in
such a loving, caring way. He cancels our sins and wraps
His arms of love around us and welcomes us back into His
presence. He is not a God who heaps condemnation upon us.

Instead He understands and welcomes us back. Never be afraid of the kind of reception you will receive when you come home to the Father.

Haman had opened the door to evil. He had allowed pride and ego to take control. What he did not yet realise was that this would be his downfall. As the song ends, Mordecai approaches Haman and stares him in the face, refusing to bow down. Haman cannot believe his insolence and leaves in a furious rage.

Bible Study Notes

Read Esther 3:1–6

1. Haman allowed pride and ego to be the doorway to evil in his life. Write down/discuss how can we avoid this in our lives?

2. What can we learn from the fact that Mordecai did not bow down to Haman?

3. Hidden sins tie our hands and our hearts. Meditate on 1 John 1:9. Write down/discuss what you receive from this verse.

4. Read Romans 13:11–14 and write down what God says to you through this passage. Think through what it means to "clothe yourselves with the Lord Jesus Christ" and what difference that makes to your everyday life.

Chapter 8

The Edict

Different; Different; Different

There are a certain people in your Kingdom who are different, their customs are different, they are a dangerous people; they must be destroyed. They are ... different.

As Mordecai stands on stage, pictures and sounds of war and genocide appear on the screen. The music of "The Edict", written by Andy Hunter reverberates around the hall. The words "different", "dangerous" and "destroy" invade our senses as Haman talks to the King. He knows what he is trying to achieve. He not only wants Mordecai killed, but he wants the whole nation destroyed. His words are very persuasive:

"There are a certain people dispersed and scattered throughout your Kingdom. These people are different to us; their customs are different and they do not obey the King's laws. It is not in the King's best interest to tolerate

them. They are different! They must be destroyed. If it
pleases the King, let a decree be issued to destroy them. I'll
put money into the pot for the men who carry out this
business."

(See Esther 3:8–9)

The King is deceived into thinking that these people are a
threat to him and to his nation. He doesn't want a dangerous
people living in his land and so he issues the order and tells
Haman, "Keep your money and do with this people whatever
you please" (Esther 3:11).

Haman decides that the annihilation of the Jews will take
place on a single day. He writes an edict that all Jews, young
and old, men, women and little children, will all die on the
thirteenth month of Adar and not only that but the Persian
population can take over their property and claim their goods.

As Mordecai watches the screen, he cannot believe what he
is seeing and hearing. His nation is about to be destroyed. He
and his people are going to be murdered. Images of destruction and desolation fill the screen. Mordecai sinks to the
ground in horror and despair. What can be done?

As Mordecai rises slowly and Esther and her two attendants
appear, a text message from Esther appears on the screen:

What is wrong? Why are you crying?

Mordecai texts a message to Esther that the whole Jewish
nation will be destroyed and urges her to go to the King.
Esther replies saying it would be madness to go into the King's
presence without being summoned. The law is that anyone
who appears before the King without being summoned must
be put to death, the only exception to this is if the King holds
out the gold sceptre. If this happens then the life is spared.
Mordecai replies, "Do not think that because you are in the
King's house that you alone of all the Jews will escape. Maybe

you have come to the kingdom for such a time as this" (Esther 4:12–14).

As the text finishes, dark figures representing death appear on stage and cross the podium towards Esther and Mordecai. They feel surrounded by the oppression that fills the air. They are both in despair. What can be done? How can we survive?

Throughout history the "spirit of Haman" has risen to the surface consistently and even today our news reports that this "spirit of evil" is still alive and well. You can't help but think of people like Corrie ten Boom, Oscar Schindler or Raoul Wallenberg who risked their own lives, like Esther, to save the Jews. Throughout history, again and again, we see people stand and rise in the middle of intense hatred to make a difference. It has been said that evil triumphs when good men do nothing. Whether it's in times of persecution or not, God is looking for "Esthers" who will rise up and make a difference.

Are you ready to make a difference for God? Are you ready to stand up and be counted? It's so easy to ignore what we see in our newspapers and what we see and hear on our television screens. Many thousands are dying each day because of poverty, the effects of war, natural disasters and diseases like AIDS, yet it is all too easy for us to ignore the cries of the poor, broken and lost.

In 2004, I had the privilege of visiting Uganda with Christian Aid to make a film about the many who live with HIV / AIDS. What I saw has left an imprint on my life that will never go away. I could not believe the poverty I saw. I had seen the pictures on television, but there is nothing like seeing it first hand for yourself. I met so many desperate people. Let me tell you about one lady who I will never forget. Jane was 52 years of age, yet she looked at least 70. She was so ill with the effects of AIDS that she could not get up off the floor. On the day we arrived to visit her she had no food to eat and no prospect of getting any. We took an offering from what we had and that gave her enough food to last her and her family for a month.

As we sat on the dirt floor and talked I discovered that her husband had died from the effects of AIDS just months previously. There was no furniture, not even a bed, all she had was a dirt floor on which to rest her weary head, yet she told me excitedly of how God had provided her with this mud hut. She had given her life to Jesus a number of months previously and her face positively glowed with His love. As we continued to talk, she was more concerned about the fact that a small insect had crawled on to my arm than she was about her surroundings. As she gently lifted it off my arm, I realised that although she lived in such adverse poverty, she was rich in the love of God. I told her I would never forget her and I know I never will. My prayer every day is, "Lord, don't let me forget Jane and the many thousands like her." It is so easy to close our minds to the many issues that affect our world today. Let's not close our eyes or bury our heads in the sand, but let's stand up where we are and make a difference for God.

Mordecai and Esther were going through a horrendous time. The news was that unless God stepped in their whole nation was going to be destroyed. This part in the show is designed to show that our nation too will be destroyed unless God steps in. There are many in our nation that do not know the love of God and do not know that they are on a journey to a lost eternity. Ray based this part of the show on William Booth's vision of many thousands drowning in the rough seas whilst the Church sits on the rock and discusses whether we should hold out a hand and save some poor soul from drowning. Whilst watching this part of the show, I personally cannot help but intercede for many who are hurting, for the needy and the lost. There is a way of escape if you and I will only take up the challenge and allow God to use us.

As the figures of death disappear from stage, Mordecai and Esther take centre stage and sing a duet which shows the depth of their relationship. Mordecai puts forward to Esther what is on his mind, but Esther's words betray her fears.

Bible Study Notes

Read Esther 3:12 – 4:8

1. Mordecai responded to the edict by praying, fasting, mourning and crying bitterly. Write down or discuss what you can learn from his response.

2. There are still so many cruel injustices happening in our world, yet how many of us pray and weep over them? Think through/discuss what you can do personally to change the world we live in.

3. Meditate on Matthew 5:13 and write down/discuss what you receive through this.

4. Memorise Matthew 5:10: "Blessed are those who are persecuted because of righteousness, for theirs is the kingdom of heaven."

Chapter 9

Will You Be the One?

Mordecai sings:
You're one of us, altogether lost
You won't escape the holocaust
It won't go away, can't you hear the cries
Their fading hope of freedom dies
You're in the perfect place
Come on girl, don't hide your face

Will you be the one who stands up strong?
Will you be the one who carries on
Oh don't turn away
I need to see you walk on through the door
Even though my heart says please don't go
You know there's no other way

Esther replies:
Don't you know what you are asking me to do?
Such a risk, a risk to take for you
I can't walk in just to say hello
My world will end (if he says no)
Give me some time and space
I have to find some saving grace.

Written by Ray Goudie/Mark Underdown/Mark Vallance
Published by Curious? Music UK/ngm/Copyright Control © 2005

As the first few words are sung you realise that in this song Mordecai is pleading with Esther not to ignore the circumstances. He says, "Esther, the situation won't go away – you are in a perfect place to do something about it. Come on girl, don't hide your face." Esther responds by saying, "Don't you know what you are asking me to do? It's such a risk to take for you. I can't walk in and just say hello. My life will end if he says no."

Esther is struggling with the "**I, me and my**" factor. "Mordecai, don't you realise that **I** may be killed? **I** can't just walk in there and put **my** case before Xerxes. He would have **my** head off before **I** can utter a word. **I** don't think **I** can do anything to help." She cannot see the bigger picture. All she can see is what might happen to her. Mordecai tries to help her to see things correctly. "Do not think for a moment that because you are in the King's house you alone of all the Jews will escape." In other words, "Esther you are one of us – a Jew – you won't escape even if you are in the Palace. Instead of protecting yourself, don't you see you are in a perfect place to make a difference? You could possibly save a nation from destruction. Don't turn away, Esther. Don't you see this could be your destiny?" He then goes on to say, "Esther if you remain silent at this time, relief and deliverance for the Jews will arise from another place but you and your father's family will perish. And who knows but that you have come to royal position for such a time as this" (Esther 4:12–14).

When disasters happen to us, we are often taken up with how this change or disaster will affect me or my family and friends. It's often very helpful to ask God to begin to let you see the problem from His perspective and when you do, you often begin to see things in a completely different light.

Have you ever felt that the disaster, problem or difficulty that has happened is just too big for you to deal with? Jesus tells us in the Bible not to worry and yet we live in a world full of fear, worry and stress. Have you ever noticed too how things often seem worse in the night? One night after hours of needless worry, with my brain sore from thinking through the many issues, I said to Jesus, "Lord, I give You all my concerns; just let me rest my weary head on You." In my imagination, I saw myself lay my head on His chest. As I did so, my whole body relaxed and I fell fast asleep. When I woke up in the morning, the issues were still there, but I knew that God was with me. Whether the issues are huge or not, instead of worrying, take your problems, fears, concerns and difficulties to God. He is more than capable, as we will see through the story of Esther, of working out our troubles and trials. He has answers when we have none.

Throughout this *Luv Esther* project alone, Ray and I have often felt that the problems seemed too big. There have been many concerns and difficult situations and at times it has been difficult to keep our eyes on the Lord rather than on the circumstances. At one point in the journey when we thought it was all going ahead smoothly, suddenly something happened that caused us to fall flat on our faces before God again. We had to go back to God with some financial pressures (some funding we thought was secure was suddenly put on hold) which led us to say, "What should we do now, Lord? Is *Luv Esther* finished?" We were just going on holiday when we heard the devastating news. What was supposed to be a few precious days of rest and relaxation with our family, quickly sunk into a number of hours and days of worry and concern. Ray had to phone someone who we were in the process of hiring to administrate the tour and let him know that we could no longer proceed. It was a horrible time. We began to question God, "Do you want this production to go ahead Lord? Is *Luv Esther* in your plans for us?" Days of seeking God's will were followed by an assurance that God was in this project and He would bring it into being. The financial difficulties were still there but we proceeded with peace in our hearts knowing that somehow our faithful God would overcome the problems. Whatever circumstances you face in life, trust God to work them out for you. He does not promise that life will be rosy, but he does promise that He will be with you (Deuteronomy 31:8).

At times, throughout the journey of *Luv Esther*, it seemed as if we would overcome one problem and then go straight into another. On the day of the Première at the Colston Hall in Bristol, we were so beset by problems and difficulties that it seemed as though we would have to cancel the event that evening. During the day, as the crew set up, we discovered that the programming for the lights had been "lost" which meant hours of reprogramming without the main programmer being there. The video is of paramount importance to the show and during the day we discovered that the projector was not working. We also managed for a time to misplace the star cloth which is part of the scenery at the back of stage.

The tickets for that evening's show had been completely sold out and we had hired the Colston Hall for the following evening to have Première 2. On the first evening we had invited over one hundred VIPs to view the show, many of whom were either parents/friends of the cast, or were people who had or would invest financially in the project. There were also invited guests who would perhaps book the show to come to their area. We had to make sure the show was the best it could be, but I could tell from the many manic phone calls from Ray, that it was only God's grace that we could rely on. Through prayer and faith in God and our workers, we managed to overcome virtually every problem that arose, but there was a close call during the afternoon when the performance was very nearly called off. You can imagine the pressure that Ray in particular went through as the producer/writer. What could we do? We could do nothing, other than give the whole pressure and problem over to God.

Both evenings were a huge success, thanks to our amazingly faithful Father God.

When problems seems huge and you seem very small, do remember that one person with God on their side can move a mountain; can turn the tide; can change a nation. Esther knew she could not approach the King in her own strength, but in God's strength and with His wonderful presence with her, she eventually was willing to try.

I believe God is looking for people who will ultimately respond like Esther. As I have said before God is looking for people who will stand up and make a difference in this world. There have been many in the past who have been prepared to do so like John Wesley, Smith Wigglesworth, Evan Roberts, Lord Shaftsbury, George Müller, William Wilberforce etc. Before Evan Roberts prayed his famous prayer, "Lord bend me and save the Church," he spent many a day and night in intercession before God. After he looked into the wonderful face of Jesus people said that his face glowed with God's presence. He was convinced that God was going to bring revival to his nation of Wales and was prepared to do something about it. As he put himself on the line for God, God moved in revival power and thousands of lives were transformed. William Wilberforce did not give up when his paper for the abolishment of the slave trade was rejected by parliament fifteen times. It was only after thirty-seven years of not giving up that he finally had success and saw Britain and her colonies abolish the slave trade.

Are you ready to respond and say, "I will do whatever it takes to see my nation saved by the power of God"? God wants you to make a difference right where you are, whether that is in politics, the media, in business, or on the streets. Will you stand up strong and dare to make a difference?

The question hanging in the air as Mordecai leaves Esther alone on stage is will she take up her destiny and stand up for what is right?

Bible Study Notes

Read Esther 4:9–14

1. During these few verses we see again how important it is to have a godly mentor in our lives. When Esther could not see things correctly, Mordecai was there to show her which road she should choose. What can we learn from this? Think through/discuss the importance of having a mentor.

2. Esther knew she could not change things on her own, but with God's help she could move mountains. Meditate on Philippians 4:13 and write down/discuss what you learn from this verse.

3. Memorise Philippians 4:19: "I can do everything through him who gives me strength."

4. The challenge of Mordecai resonates with us, the Church, today. Will we stand up for the poor and for those who have no voice? Find some verses that show God's heart for the poor and ask God to show you how you can step out of your comfort zone and make a difference.

Chapter 10

For This Very Moment

For this very moment
Is this why I am here?
To stand up and be counted
And to reach beyond my fear
I don't want to drink this cup of sacrifice
Do I have to throw this final roll of the dice?
Yet I can't just walk away
And if I die ... I die.

Written by Ray Goudie/Chris Eaton (West Lodge Music/Here's To Jo)
Published by Curious? Music UK/ngm/SGO Publishing Ltd © 2005

What will Esther do? Will she ignore what Mordecai has said? Can she face and confront the powerful, despicable Haman? Is her voice going to make one bit of difference? She knows that the laws of Persia and Media once made cannot be repealed (Esther 1:19), so what can she do? How can she make a difference?

It is at this point in the story that you realise that Esther has a huge choice to make. She can either ignore what Mordecai has said or she can take all the courage she has, which is virtually non-existent, and confront the issue of Haman. She knows very clearly that if she goes in to see the King without being asked, then she risks being killed. She was not being melodramatic. It was a very real threat to her life. After all, this was the King who banished and possibly executed his wife, Vashti, for her refusal to obey one command.

Mordecai had reminded Esther, "Who knows, maybe you have been called for such a time as this," and as she sings the main ballad of the show the thoughts going around in her head echo around the theatre:

> For this very moment,
> Is this why I am here?
> To stand up and be counted
> And to reach beyond my fear.

"Is this why God put me in the palace – for such a time as this?" she asks herself. "Can God use me, little me, an orphan refugee? Will anything I do make a difference?"

And still she sings on:

> I don't want to drink this cup of sacrifice
> Do I have to throw this final roll of the dice?
> Yet I can't just walk away

She was struggling with drinking the cup prepared for her. Many years later, when Jesus was going through His last lonely night in Gethsemane He too struggled with the cup He had to drink. Jesus knew that God the Father could remove this cup from Him, but He also knew that if He chose not to go through the pain of the cross, then our salvation would not have come. It is only possible for us to come to know the Father and spend eternity with Him because Jesus drank that bitter cup right to the last drop. Jesus clearly stated to His Father God, "Not my will, but yours be done." On the cross,

Jesus lifted up His voice and shouted, "It is finished." In other words, "**I have completed all You have told Me to do. I have done it! Salvation is complete**." Esther had her own struggle with God, but at the end of the day she said, "I have chosen to do Your will, O Lord!"

> Yet I can't just walk away.
> And if I die, I die.

Esther eventually reckoned that even though she was only one person standing against the wickedness of Haman, if God was with her then that was more than enough. She calls upon Mordecai and the rest of the Jews in Susa to fast for three days and three nights, while she and her maids do the same. She says in Esther 4:16, "When this is done, I will go to the king, even though it is against the law. And if I perish, I perish."

As I write this, I am reminded of the story in the Bible where the King of Aram is at war with Israel. Every time the King of Aram makes a move, the King of Israel seems to know about it. The King of Aram is furious and wants to know who is informing the King of Israel of his plans. His people tell him that it is the prophet Elisha and so he sends his armies to capture him. Elisha and his servant come out of their home one morning to discover a massive army surrounding their city. Elisha's servant panics and says, "Oh my Lord, what shall we do?" Elisha, however, is not fazed by all the thousands of enemy soldiers who are against him. He knows he is only one person, but with God's help he can win the day. Elisha replies, "Don't be afraid, those who are with us are more than those who are with them." Elisha then prays for his servant's eyes to be opened, and when his servant looks he sees the hills full of horses and chariots of fire all around Elisha. When he saw how many of God's forces were with Elisha I am sure a smile slowly appeared on his face.

We often forget that we are not alone. Esther was relying on the faithfulness of God. She was only one person but she had the Hosts of Heaven with her. She may not be able to see them, but as she would walk into the throne room to confront Haman, she would not walk in alone.

God may never ask us to do what Esther did, but He will ask us to take huge steps of faith as we walk through life with Him. It's in those moments that we need to remember we are not taking these faith steps on our own, but that Heaven is standing with us and cheering us on. God calls us every day to take up our "cross" and follow Him. 2 Corinthians 4:1 says, "We always carry around in our body the death of Jesus, so that the life of Jesus may also be revealed in our body." In other words, we choose to lay down our lives for Jesus. We choose to kill off the self-life so that Jesus' life can be seen in us. We choose every day to be laid-down lovers of Jesus. He is the One that is important; He's the One we want to please.

As the curtain falls on the first half of the musical Luv Esther and the applause from the audience ends, the words "and if I die, I die!" seem to still reverberate around the hall. Esther was prepared to put her life on the line – are you? Are you prepared to trust God for your future? Do you want to become a laid-down lover of Jesus?

Bible Study Notes

Read Esther 4:15–17

1. Esther was prepared to put herself on the altar and die to self. In what areas of your own life do you find it difficult to die to self?

2. Paraphrase Galatians 2:20 – in other words put the verse into your own words. Write down what you learn through doing this.

3. Meditate on Philippians 3:10 and write down/discuss
    what you receive through this.

4. Spend time praying and giving yourself wholly to God
    again just like Esther did. Willingly embrace all that
    God has for you.

Photos from
Luv Esther

Esther in preparation to meet the King

Mordecai wonders, "What does this all mean?"

The hopefuls look to join the royal scene

Hegai the royal eunuch played by George Mhondera

The cast perform "Everybody's Talking"

Esther the bride

The wicked Haman and his entourage

Haman performing the
song "Don't You Know
Who I Am?"

Celebrating the great Salvation Day

Ray Goudie and Murray Watts at the rehearsals

ACT TWO

Chapter 11

Throne Room Party

Come on let's have some fun and celebrate
And dance to the music tonight
Come on and raise your glass and make some noise
And set your heart and soul alight
Oh what a loving feeling's come to me
Come on and feel the rhythm inside
My body's moving and I just can't stop
I never wanna say goodbye

I can feel the love from you, you're everything
I can feel the love from you, so amazing.

Written by Ray Goudie/Kevan Frost
Published by Curious? Music UK/ngm © MCS Music Ltd © 2005

The second half of the musical *Luv Esther* bursts open with the cast and Hegai dancing and singing in the throne room. It's a celebration of the King's love and favour.

When Ray wrote this song, he wanted to portray that when we go into the throne room of the King of kings we are entering a place where there is much fun, joy and laughter. When Ray was young he had the impression that Heaven was a very quiet place where everyone was very emotionless and solemn. It was only as he began to explore the Bible and began to know God for himself that he realised that to be in God's presence meant the biggest party and celebration ever. In the book of Revelation, it actually records that there was silence in Heaven for thirty minutes. Why would John write that there was a period of extended silence if silence is the norm in Heaven? The song, "Throne Room Party" expresses a little of what it is like to be in the presence of the King. To look on His face; to behold His glory; to realise afresh His amazing love for us means that you cannot help but be filled with an inexpressible joy.

> I feel alive 'cause I'm having such a good time, a good time
> I can't believe that I'm dancing with you such a good time,
> a good time
> Over and over my mind is exploding a good time,
> a good time
> Everyone's turning around and around such a good time,
> a good time

Through this song we can see that the reason there is much joy is because the throne room is where we can find the King. Obviously King Xerxes does not even begin to compare with the King of kings, Jesus, and in many ways he was the complete opposite. But, when we really fall in love with Jesus, we just cannot wait to be in His presence, to be in His throne room, to worship and adore Him, to be near Him is all we desire. The song states,

> I never wanna say goodbye

and that is so true. You never want to leave His tangible presence. You never want to leave Him, not for a second because He is so wonderful. When you discover what it is like to lie at His feet, to look into His eyes; to dance and to sing with Him, to hear Him say that He is wild about you, you never want to leave. Nothing else compares with Jesus. His love is beyond our wildest dreams. Nothing is more important. Let me ask you a question? Have you fallen in love with Jesus? Have you discovered that when you come into His throne room there is great joy? Do you know that He loves you so much? Have you looked into His eyes and been wrecked with His love? Have you responded to Him when He has asked you to dance with Him in His throne room?

Just recently I prayed for a lady who desperately needed a touch of the love of God. She had many problems and difficulties in her life and didn't know which way to turn. As I prayed for her, she saw herself enter into the throne room. When she saw the Lord, He had such compassion and love for her that it overwhelmed her. He took her by the hand and whispering in her ear, spoke of His immense love for her. With tears running down her face, she saw herself dance with Him and before long she was totally captivated by Him. Nothing else mattered if she had Jesus with her.

The Apostle Paul tells us in Ephesians that his prayer is that "we may have power together with all the saints to grasp how wide and long and high and deep is the love of Christ, and to know this love that surpasses knowledge."

Oh, we so need to know how much we are loved and accepted by God. Each time I meditate on the love of God, He brings me back to a scene I have seen many times. If I close my eyes I can see myself standing on the shore looking out on a beautiful ocean. The sea appears huge, very wide and very deep. As I look to the horizon, it does not seem to end. As I take in this wonderful picture, I hear the words, "Nancy, My love for you is much deeper than the biggest ocean; it is much wider than the sky. There is no end to My love for you. Dive into My love for My love for you is beyond anything you have ever known or ever experienced."

God loves each of us so much. Do you know His love for you will never end? Do you know that you are so special to Him? Never underestimate how much God loves you and wants you to be with Him. He loves you with a faithful and everlasting love. It does not matter who you are or what has happened in your life, God loves you and will continue to love you. Today, why don't you discover how much God loves you and let that knowledge free you to enter into His courts with joy and thanksgiving. Come on – let's have some fun and celebrate with our wonderful King – Jesus!

As Hegai and the dancers leave the stage, the mood changes dramatically to portray a sense of fear and awe. What is going to happen? As Esther prepares to enter the throne room, will she be accepted by the King or will she die?

Bible Study Notes

Read Esther 5:1

1. Think through/discuss the kind of emotions that Esther would have been experiencing as she walked towards the throne room. Think through/discuss what emotions you experience as you think about meeting Jesus in Heaven. Write down/discuss what you can learn from this.

2. John 3:16 tells us that God loves each of us so much that He was willing to sacrifice His all so that you and I might live with Him in eternity. Jeremiah 31:3 tells us that the Lord loves us with an everlasting love. Think back over your life and write down/discuss when and where you felt the love of God for you.

3. Read 1 Peter 1:8. Are you filled with an inexpressible and glorious joy? We describe it as having a "Woohoo" in our hearts. Ask God to wake you up to His amazing love and allow His joy to permeate your life.

4. Meditate on Isaiah 51:11 and write down/discuss what you receive from this.

Chapter 12

Throne Room Glory/
Throne Room Love

Don't do it! Don't do it! You'll die! You'll die!

As the haunting music to "Throne Room Glory" fills the theatre, you see Esther preparing herself to enter the King's presence. There are many voices whispering to her, "Don't do it! Don't do it! Don't go to the King! Don't do it! You'll die! You'll die!" But she carries on nonetheless and approaches the throne room. The words Holy, Holy, Holy echo throughout the theatre. It's as if Esther is entering into the most holy place. There's a sense of awe, fear and anticipation. She falls flat on her face before the King, her body draped over the stairs of the set. As the song reaches its climax, the King sees Esther and his response is recorded for us in Esther 5:2. "When he [the King] saw Queen Esther standing in the court, he was pleased with her and held out to her the gold sceptre that was in his hand. So Esther approached and touched the tip of the sceptre."

What a wonderful picture of coming into the presence of King Jesus. As we approach His throne we know we are entering into the Holy of Holies and the only thing we can do is to fall on our faces before Him. When He sees us He is pleased with us and runs to us. It is obvious that He wants us with Him. The throne room is a place of acceptance and warmth; a place where we will never be turned away. We should never fear the response from our God. He loves us and will always love us and no matter who we are He will always have a huge welcome for us.

When Jesus came to this earth, He came to show the world just how much the Father loves us. One of my favourite stories of Jesus clearly outlines God's love for us. Jesus told a story which is recorded in Luke 15 of two young men, one of whom was desperate to have his inheritance from his Father. He could not wait until his Father died, he wanted his inheritance and he wanted it now, so he went to his dad and asked him for it. The Father loved his son so much that he gave him what he asked for. The son immediately went off and spent the money on wine, women and song. Everyone was his friend while he had money, but when the money ran out, no one wanted to know him. He had no food, however he managed to get a job feeding some pigs and the Bible says that he longed to fill his stomach with what the pigs were eating.

When he was at his lowest, he suddenly came to his senses. He said to himself, "This is ridiculous, I will go back to my father's house where there is lots of food and ask my father to make me one of his hired servants." So he started on his journey home. The Bible says that while he was still a long way off, the Father who had never stopped looking for his boy to return, saw him and ran to him. He kissed him and he hugged him. The delight of the father was evident for all to see. The son could not get all his words out before the father was asking for new clothes for him. He put a ring on his finger signifying that he was his son. The father did not make him a servant, he restored him to his place as his son. He killed the fatted calf and they had a party. You see, the father loved him so much and was so pleased that his son had come back. It did

not matter how much he had hurt him, deserted him or used
him, he was just so pleased to have him back with him. That's
how much our God loves us. It does not matter what we have
done in our past, when we return to God, He is overjoyed to
see us. There is always a huge loving welcome for each of us.

In the throne room, the King starts to sing:

Throne Room Love

I just can't believe my eyes
Can't believe you're really here
Like a dream coming true
You awaken all my love
I give it all to you

What do you want me to do for you?
Rise up my lover and come to me
What do you want me to do for you?
I want to hold you in my arms

Esther replies:

Give me once glance of your eyes
Just a kiss all fears fly away

Will you come so close to me
Let me whisper in your ear
All I want, my desire
Is to be with you my love
Share the secrets of my heart

Your majesty
Your majesty
I lay my life before you
I love you, majesty
Give me once glance of your eyes
Just a kiss all fears fly away

The King responds:

> Like a star you shine so clear
> Like a jewel so precious to me
> Hold my hand I'll take you high
> Like an angel's wings
> We can fly, we can soar

They both sing:

> Your majesty
> What do you want me to do for you?
> Your majesty
> Rise up my lover and come to me
> I lay my life before you
> I love you, Majesty
> I want to hold you in my arms
> Give me once glance of your eyes
> Just a kiss all fears will fly away

> Written by Ray Goudie/Mark Vallance/Will Rowe
> Published by Curious? Music UK/ngm/Copyright control © 2005

After accepting Esther into his presence, the King's question was, "What do you want me to do for you, Esther? Even if you request half my kingdom, I will give it to you!" What a wonderful picture of our God. He pours out His love and acceptance to us, but more than that, He is so amazingly generous with us. King Xerxes said he would give her up to half of his kingdom if she requested it. That wasn't the kind of response she was expecting, but money, position or power was not on her agenda that day.

I have discovered throughout years of "living by faith" for our finances that God is incredibly generous, much more so than any earthly employer would ever be.

I remember during our first year of full-time Christian work someone being surprised that we should be able to take a holiday. They said, "I didn't think missionaries had holidays, but only took furloughs, and even then they travel the country telling others about their work." I also remember being told that we would never have a lovely home now that we were in full-time Christian work. People felt we had given up so much, but we felt as though we had given up so little. We had left our home, our friends, our church, our jobs, even our nation and followed God into the unknown. We went to live in one of the worst cities in our land and slept in a home in the red-light district and yet we were happy, excited and contented, because we knew we were doing what God had called us to do. Throughout the years God has remained faithful to us. We have had an amazing life serving Jesus. There have been many sacrifices that we have had to make, but as we do it gladly, God pours out His love and favour on us. We are never the losers. We have flown on a private Lear Jet; we have received a gift of a special holiday to Mauritius; we have skied in Colorado; all of which we would not have done if we had not followed Jesus and trusted Him for everything we need. If I had my life to live again, choosing to follow Jesus and do His will is something I would do all over again, even if there weren't any material blessings. Our God is most generous, but when you look into the eyes of Jesus everything else pales into insignificance.

"Throne Room Love" is a song that will always remain special to me. At my Spiritual Health conference in 2005, God revealed Himself to me through this song. On the Saturday evening after our delicious meal, 420 conference delegates plus our team gathered to watch a short cameo of Ray's musical. It was the first time that our team had performed *Luv Esther* and so you can imagine the excitement and the natural anxiety that was in the air. Ray had let me listen to "Throne Room Love" many times and I knew that it represented us going into the throne room to be with Jesus.

As this song was performed, I was transported into the throne room of the King of kings. I could hear Jesus saying, "Nancy, what do you want Me to do for you?" I could feel His amazing love and sense His deep warmth for me. As I stood in front of Jesus I could not hold back the tears of joy that poured from my eyes. I had never experienced His love so much. I glanced into His eyes and I was immediately washed in His sea of love. What joy filled my heart!

When you glance into His eyes you are not afraid to be completely abandoned in His arms. Let Him kiss you with His love and it will transform your life. I felt God kiss me that night and His kisses felt more delightful than wine (Song of Songs 1:2). He drew me deeper than ever before and said, "Come, my darling, my beautiful one, come with me" (Song of Songs 2:13). I was completely lost in His love. I looked into His eyes and I was beautifully undone. I fell in love with Him all over again.

Right now, hear God ask you, "What do you want Me to do for you?" May your response be the same as Esther's in the song: "I only want one glance of Your eyes, just a kiss and all fears fly away." Let Him kiss you with the kisses of His mouth and awaken His love within you. You will never be the same again!

When the King asked Esther what he could do for her, her only request was that the King and Haman would dine with her that day. It is interesting to note as we leave this scene, that although Esther had been fasting, consuming no food or water for three days, at the same time she had been planning a banquet. Many people, when they are fasting, feel that they cannot cope with talking about food, never mind preparing a banquet fit for a King. Esther is an amazing lady!

At the banquet, the King once more asks Esther, "What is your petition?" He again offers her up to half of his kingdom, but her only response is, "Would you and Haman please come and dine with me again tomorrow? Then I will answer the King's question" (Esther 5:6–7). As Haman leaves the first banquet he walks out with a spring in his step. He thinks to himself, "Well, I have really made it now. I'm the only one to be invited to Queen Esther's banquet with the King. No-one can stop me now. I've made it to the top."

Bible Study Notes

Read Esther 5:2–8

1. Verses 2–3 tell us how much the King loved Esther. Look for a verse in the Bible that tells you how much you are loved and spend time thanking God for His amazing love for you.

2. Esther received a wonderful welcome from the King. The prodigal son received an amazing welcome from his father. What kind of welcome do you anticipate receiving when you come into God's presence and why?

3. The King asked Esther, "What do you want me to do for you? What is your request?" If Jesus were to stand in front to you right now and ask you the same question – what would you say? Think through/discuss your answers.

4. Meditate on Ephesians 1:3–4 and write down/discuss what you receive from this. What does this tell us about God's generosity towards us?

Chapter 13

Who Can Stop Me Now?

Who can stop me now?
I've made it to the top
Who can stop me?
Who can stop me?
Who can stop me now?
I'm in the centre spot
Who can stop me?
Who can stop me?
I've made it to the top

One thing that makes me angry
That really gets me down
Is why that one man will not bow
And let me wear my crown

You're a man of power
The world is in your hands
You should build the biggest stage
And on it hang the man

Written by Ray Goudie/Mark Vallance/Kevan Frost
Published by Curious? Music UK/ngm/copyright Control/© MCS Music

As he leaves the King and Queen after the first banquet, Haman's joy is short-lived as he sees his hated enemy sitting at the King's gate. When he notices that Mordecai does not bow to him or show any fear in his presence, he fills with rage against Mordecai (Esther 5:9) and goes home to share his fury and his joy with his wife and friends. He gathers all his friends together and says, "Hey, let me tell you what has happened to me – I've really made it now."

> I've even got the queen on board
> She wants my autograph

However,

> One thing that makes me angry
> That really gets me down
> Is why that one man will not bow
> And let me wear my crown

His wife, Zeresh, says:

> You're a man of power
> The world is in your hands
> You should build the biggest stage
> And on it hang the man

This suggestion delights Haman and there and then he gives the order to build the biggest gallows ever. He will hang Mordecai on it, if it is the last thing he does.

As Haman and the dancers leave the stage, Hegai comes back to tell us of a bizarre turn of events:

> Evil has a way of working through the night
> Haman is going to make Mordecai pay like today

But there is one little problem, something is bothering
   the King
And he just can't sleep
They bring him the royal diaries and as he flips through
   the pages,
Bang! There it is!
The case of Mordecai unmasking the murderous plot of
   Bigthan and Teresh.
Has anything been done to honour this hero?
The answer, zero!
Just then, Haman comes up the stairs ready to propose
   the execution of Mordecai as a solution
Check the twist in the tale and a neat resolution.

Again, we notice the "Unseen Conductor" bringing all the "instruments" in at the right time. The King could not sleep that night and so asks for the history books to be opened. He particularly wants to read the account of his reign. As the times and events are being read to him, he realises that nothing has been done for Mordecai who has exposed Bigthan and Teresh's plot to assassinate him. He immediately wants to put that right. Right on cue, Haman enters the outer court of the King to speak to the King about hanging Mordecai. Now who could have engineered these kinds of circumstances coming together at the right time? No-one could have done this, but God.

Before Haman can utter a word, the voice of the King fills the air. "What shall be done for the man whom the King delights to honour?" Haman's pride makes him wrongly conclude that this could only be him.

It can only be me! Me! Me! It must be me!

Haman's voice immediately fills the stage. "**The man the King delights to honour? It must be me! Me! Me, Haman!**

It must be me, Haman!" The name and face of Haman fills the screen. He imagines the newspaper reports all over the Kingdom. The story of **Haman** – featuring **Haman!** The golden Grammy award goes to **Haman!** Tonight the Oscar goes to **Haman!** The thought of it being anyone else did not occur to him. He approaches the King and says, "For the man the King delights to honour, have them bring a royal robe the King has worn and a horse the King has ridden, one with a royal crest placed on its head. Then let the robe and horse be entrusted to one of the King's most noble princes. Let them robe the man and lead him on the horse through the city streets, proclaiming before him, 'This is what is done for the man the King delights to honour!' "

The King thinks that Haman's suggestion is an excellent idea and then declares that Haman should do this for Mordecai the Jew. The words, "Mordecai the Jew", echo throughout the theatre. Haman is left in torment. Mordecai the Jew? Oh no, this is the worst thing that could have happened! I cannot believe this! How did this happen?

Haman's worst nightmare is soon realised. He is forced to clothe Mordecai in the King's royal robe and put him on the King's horse and lead him through the streets saying, "This is what is done for the man the King delights to honour."

On the screen, the newspaper headlines and the television and radio programmes tell the story of how Mordecai has been honoured. Finally, Haman is left on stage alone. His dreams of glory are shattered. A tortured and twisted remix of the song, "Don't You Know Who I Am" starts up again. He rushes home to tell his wife and friends of his anguish, hoping for some comfort, but his wife states prophetically, "Since Mordecai is of Jewish origin, you cannot stand against him – you will surely come to ruin!" (Esther 6:13).

Isn't it wonderful to know that even in the most difficult circumstances, God is working behind the scenes to bring His will into being? I'm sure like me, you have encountered situations in your life where it seems like all is lost and there is nothing you can do about it. I've discovered through the years that when the only thing you can hold on to is God, that's a good place to be. If God is on your side, you need not worry. God is more than capable of bringing victory out of seeming defeat.

During the years 1996–2001 we went through a walk of faith to trust God for a Missions and Arts centre. It is an amazing story of God's faithfulness to us which you can read in my book called *H.O.T. Faith** Throughout the whole walk of faith there were many times where it seemed as though we would never see God's word fulfilled, yet as we kept on believing Him through the tough circumstances, God did miracle after miracle. At one point in the journey, we were in the process of buying the property and the land when the sellers mysteriously pulled out. Ray was in Germany at the time when I received the phone call. As you can imagine we were both devastated, but there was nothing we could do other than pray. As I prayed God gave me a specific verse of Scripture and I asked God to confirm it by giving the same scripture to Ray in Germany. When I phoned Ray later and told him I had a verse from God, I discovered that God had given him the exact same word. We knew God was with us and that helped us to continue to believe that He would somehow turn the situation around. In the natural it looked as though the deal was completely dead, but after a weekend of prayer and holding on to God's word, we received a phone call on the Monday morning telling us that the sale was miraculously back on.

If God had not acted, Mordecai's life could have been ended. Instead God turned the situation around in seconds. That's the kind of God we have. It does not matter what is going on in your life, our God is able to change circumstances

* Nancy Goudie, *H.O.T. Faith*, Sovereign World, 2004.

in a second if He chooses to do so. There's a story which is told in 2 Kings 6 – 7 where the nation of Israel is surrounded by its enemies. Great fear, desperation and famine grip the people of Israel. One man after hearing a prophecy that God was going to bring salvation for Israel said, "Look, even if God were to open the floodgates of the heavens, could this happen?" Within a few short hours, God had completely changed the situation. In the night, their enemies thought they were being attacked and ran off leaving all their food and possessions. In the morning, God had done that which was thought to be impossible. Is there a situation which seems impossible to you? The story of Esther shows us that our God is able to deal with any situation that arises in our lives.

Bible Study Notes

Read Esther 5:9–14 and 6:1–14

1. The words of the song say, "Who can stop me now?" but we know from the story of Esther that God is quite capable of stopping evil from triumphing. Write down/ discuss what happened in chapter 6 and what we can learn from this.

2. Esther trusted in God to work things out for her. Write down how easy/hard you find trusting God or others and think through/discuss your answers.

3. Memorise Proverbs 3:5–6: "Trust in the LORD with all your heart and lean not on your own understanding; in all your ways acknowledge him, and he will make your paths straight."

4. Meditate on Romans 8:28 and write down/discuss what you receive from God.

Chapter 14

The Melodrama/Save My People

A silent movie tells the story

Haman is in a mess and it's about to become an even bigger mess, but before he can think about it anymore, the King's eunuchs arrive at his home and rush him off to the second banquet.

The King and the Queen walk back on stage and are joined by Haman. Hegai arrives on stage to tell us what is happening:

> They say Esther is the queen with a perfect face
> I'm telling you straight, she's one beauty with a brain
> She's got perfect timing next time they are dining
> She's gonna prove her place in the royal esteem
> Yo she's planned the whole scene.
>
> It's time for truth, it's time for facts
> Time for justice in the face of attack
> Poor Haman aint gonna last his time over
> It's like a climax in the movies – the issue is in black
>   and white
> Check it out.

We now enter into the world of the silent movie era. Try to imagine going to the cinema in those early days where a pianist sits at the front and musically interprets the drama unfolding before him in glorious black and white. This is exactly the world that we now enter as the video screen again takes centre stage with a stunning piano accompaniment unfolding the story of the Queen's second banquet. The King once again asks Esther, "What is your request, Esther? Even if you ask for half of my kingdom I will give it to you." This time, Esther is not slow at replying. She immediately pleads with the King for her life. She says, "Grant me my life, this is my petition and spare my people, this is my request! For I and my people have been sold for destruction and slaughter and annihilation." The King responds, "Who is he? Where is the man who has dared to do such a thing?"

Esther immediately responds by condemning Haman. "The adversary and enemy is this vile and wicked Haman." You can see the terror written all over Haman's face. The King walks off in a rage and Haman knows that his days are numbered so he stays behind to beg Queen Esther for his life. Just as the King returns from his walk, Haman falls on the couch where Esther is reclining. The King is furious and says, "Will he even molest the Queen while she is with me?" As soon as the King has spoken a sack is placed over Haman's head. Then one of the King's servants tells the King that Haman has built a gallows on which he planed to hang Mordecai. The King retorts, "Then hang him on it!"

As Haman is led away to his death, again the video tells us the story. Mordecai begins to text Esther again revealing that, "The evil edict still stands ... plead with the King to save our people." The laws of the Medes and the Persians could not be changed and therefore what Haman had planned would still stand unless the King could somehow save her people.

Esther stands on stage and sings to the King:

Save my people, save my people
Reach out your hand, let freedom reign again
Save my people, save my people
Stretch out your arm, let justice rise again

I see a day
When sorrow dies
And love will say
I'm now alive
I cry to you
From deep within
Please stop the hate
So grace will win

Save my people, save my people
Reach out your hand, let freedom reign again

I hear the sound
Of silent tears
No answer found
To all their fears
I can't endure
It anymore
Let mercy sing
I now implore

Save my people, save my people
Reach out your hand, let freedom reign again
Save my people, save my people
Stretch out your arm, let justice rise again

Written by Ray Goudie/Kevan Frost
Published by Curious? Music UK/ngm/MCS Music Ltd © 2005

She pleads and intercedes before the King to do something to change these awful circumstances. "How can I bear to see disaster fall on my people? How can I bear to see the destruction of my family?" (Esther 8:6). Esther falls at his feet and pleads with tears and loud cries. Oh, how we need to intercede like this for our world. How we need to plead with God for an awakening which will deliver many thousands into the Kingdom of God. Esther was not thinking of her own life at this point, she was aware of many thousands of innocent lives who were in danger. All around us today we have nations of people who are dying both physically and spiritually.

I remember God giving me a vision whilst on mission in England which had me weeping before Him in intercession. I saw thousands and thousands of people, young and old, walking along a road not knowing that they were on their way to destruction. There was no one telling them of the danger that lay ahead. As tears poured down my face, I shared with the rest of Heartbeat what God was saying and we interceded and asked God to give us the privilege of telling people about the good news of Jesus. You see, because God loves us and because Jesus died for us, we need not go to a lost eternity. We need never be in a place where we cannot see and behold the beautiful face of Jesus.

That night as we sang in one of the local theatres which was filled with hundreds of unchurched teenagers from the local schools, the **whole** audience responded to Jesus at the appeal and hundreds gave their lives to Christ. When the minister of the church realised how many people had just responded, he grabbed the local organiser and asked, "How many Christian leaflets do you have?" He said "100!" The minister then scolded him for only having a hundred! The poor organiser had thought he was well prepared, but he had not counted on God's Spirit breaking out.

When God began to *visit* us back in 2003, we knew it was wrong to keep what we were experiencing inside the four walls of our Caedmon building. We knew God loved us and that love compelled us to reach people with the message

and love of Jesus. We couldn't just wait until people visited
ngm or came to our church building; we had to take it out to
where the lost, hurting, lonely people were. We didn't pray
and reach out to others because we knew we somehow
should, but because the love of God compelled us.

We knew that although the town we lived in was very
middle-class it was not without its problems. Many of our
teams have lived in flats in the High Street of Thornbury and
have seen first-hand the violence and fights that occur on a
Friday and Saturday night. On both of those nights each week,
the police arrive to try and deal with the under-age drinking
and the violence that happens. The drug squad try and deal
with the drug pushers who are on the streets and in the pubs.
Our nice middle-class town is often unrecognisable on Friday
and Saturday nights. We knew we needed to not only
intercede for the lost and needy but to go and reach them
ourselves. We went onto the streets, fearfully stepping into
the unknown. What would we encounter? Yet we knew we
had to go.

Every Friday night, we now hold an event called Ten/12.
Teams of us go out on the streets to invite people to our café
whilst others transform a church hall into a trendy Starbucks-
type café. When people come in we give them free coffee, hot
chocolate, biscuits, donuts and sweets and when they sit at the
tables we then put a one-on-one worker with them to chat,
build relationships and tell them about the love of Jesus. We
also have some of our singers, rappers and dj's performing
and giving testimonies throughout the night until we finish
around 12.30/1.00a.m. Each Friday night we have around
30–80 people pass through our café, many of whom have
never experienced human love, never mind the love of God.
We have opportunities to pray with many of them. Throughout the time we have done this we have seen a number of
people come to know the Lord. The first person to fall in love
with Jesus was a young fifteen-year-old girl.

When I first spoke with her on the streets she had already consumed enough alcohol to floor a grown man. She had started drinking and taking drugs when she was nine. Each weekend she would roam the streets looking for her next high. She would often end up fighting her friends. When she first visited Ten/12 she was just about to smash her friend's face in, but I managed to chat with her until her anger passed. One Friday night after she had drunk her usual bottles of vodka, Bacardi and beer we had to call an ambulance for her. One of our leaders went with her to hospital and we discovered that she had been told by her Mum that she was no longer welcome at home because of her drunken, violent behaviour. We asked the local services if they could provide her with accommodation but were told that there was none available and the only thing they could suggest was that she could sleep in a police cell for the night. We knew we could not allow that to happen to a fifteen-year-old girl, so we asked and were given permission to put her up in one of our homes. She was an alcoholic, addicted to drugs with no future to look forward to, but Jesus has changed her life. After a number of weeks, she gave her life to God, fell in love with Jesus and in her words has, "discovered the most amazing life." Without Jesus, she could easily have ended up dead. She recently celebrated her first spiritual birthday and got baptised just a number of days later.

There are many hurting and needy people all over the world who don't know that God loves them. The Lord wants us to find them and tell them about Him and intercede for them. Will you be like Esther who put her own fears behind her and sought the King's favour for her nation? Will you, like Esther, stand up and make a difference and see your nation saved? You can only do this when you are wrecked with the love of God. You will only be able to reach others for Jesus when you yourself are captivated by the love of God. You will only be able to lay down your life when your heart is pumping with passion for Jesus and compassion for the poor, the lonely and the lost. It's time to let Him kiss you with His love so that you become a radical lover who shines with Jesus no matter where you go. It's time to be an Esther.

The King then issues another edict which allows the Jews the right to assemble and protect themselves and to destroy anyone who might attack them. When the second edict was posted in every town and city there was much rejoicing. Against all the odds, salvation had come and many people's lives were saved.

Hegai comes back on stage and sums up the end of the story:

> So an edict was declared throughout the land
> Everybody was rejoicing and going crazy.
> Love coming out on top. A Nation saved.
> This is an ancient story with some minor alterations
> But it's like this:
> Evil never survives now Haman is history
> While the mystery of love blossoms like a flower.
>
> Mordecai is the man of the hour
> From doorkeeper to prime minister
> Esther, a girl in a million
> No fake or some glory snatcher
> But a true star ready to die for others
> While living as a queen.
>
> Hey get with the scene.
> We're talking love coming out on top.
> The people saved!
> Love coming out on top.
> A world to save.

Esther and Mordecai have won the day. Haman is hanged on his own gallows and Mordecai becomes the King's right-hand man. Whoever would have thought that God could do all that within such a short space of time? How amazing is our God? He turned an area of awful defeat into a wonderful victory. He can do the same for you and bring salvation to you and your family's lives.

Bible Study Notes

Read Esther 6:14 – 8:13

1. Esther was not slow in speaking when the time was right. What can we learn from this?

2. Esther 8:1 tells us that through Esther, Mordecai came into the presence of the King. Spend some time praying for friends or family that you would like to bring into the presence of the King of kings.

3. Even although Haman had exited the scene, Mordecai and Esther realised that the edict still stood. Esther again had to risk her life and beseech the King to intervene. What does this teach us about not giving up?

4. Memorise 2 Chronicles 15:7: "But as for you, be strong and do not give up, for your work will be rewarded."

Chapter 15

Salvation Day

Orders to grant all Jews in every city the right to assemble and protect themselves and to defeat any of their enemies ... order to be carried out on the thirteenth day or the twelfth month by royal decree ...

As the cast burst onto the stage, suddenly the place is filled with fun, laughter and glorious colour. An African drumbeat sounds out as the words of "Salvation Day" are sung by the whole company. The audience cannot help but be captured by the joy, passion and celebration of this salvation song.

Let the drummers take the beat
Let the rhythm sound
See the crowds of people on celebration ground
Salvation, Salvation day

Let the dance begin again
Everybody sing
Songs of liberation, let the voices ring
Salvation, salvation, salvation
Salvation, salvation day

Hear the children laughing
Hope for everyone
What a miracle amazing grace has won
Salvation, Salvation day.

Redemption written in the skies
Hope has touched our lives
We have seen the love come down on earth to all the tribes
Salvation, salvation, salvation
Salvation, salvation day.

Let the anthem ring
Tribute to the king
More than words can ever say
Oasis in the sand
The favour of his hand
We've gotta let the whole world know

Come and join the festival
Party time is here
We've seen the hand of favour let it stay with us each year
Salvation, salvation, salvation
Salvation, salvation day.

Salvation, salvation, salvation
Salvation, salvation, salvation
Salvation, salvation, salvation
Salvation, salvation, salvation

Salvation, salvation day.

Salvation, salvation day.

Let the anthem ring
Everybody sing
Let the anthem ring
Come on everybody sing.

Written by Ray Goudie/Ian White/Ian Townend/Neil Wilson
Published by Curious? Music UK/ngm/Little Misty Music © 2001

As the second edict went out across the vast nation of Persia, the Jews could not believe what their God had done. Esther 8:17 says:

"In every province and in every city, wherever the edict of the king went, there was joy and gladness among the Jews, with feasting and celebrating."

The Jews celebrated; their lives had been spared by the amazing power of God. The edict said they were allowed to protect themselves against their enemies and to kill and destroy any armed force who might attack them (Esther 8:11). The book of Esther goes on to tell us that on the thirteenth day of the twelfth month, on the day that the enemies of the Jews hoped to overpower them, the tables were turned. Esther 9:1 says that the Jews had the upper hand over those who hated them. As Murray Watts says in the *Luv Esther* programme, "The account of the destruction of the Jews' enemies as recorded in Esther 9 can make disturbing reading; however the theme of judgement must always be remembered in a world still blighted by the terrible evils of genocide." As the second edict was read and understood, mourning was turned into dancing; fear was turned into joy. An amazing miracle had happened and it was beyond their wildest dreams!

It's wonderful to know that no matter how impossible our circumstances or how difficult life is, our God can still work things out for good. He is bigger and greater than any problem we face. He is never out of resources. We may want to give up many times, but He never gives up on us. If we put our faith and trust in Him, we can, like Esther, see our circumstances completely turned around. Over the last twenty-six years in full-time Christian work, we have seen God do just that many times. We can trust Him no matter what lies ahead. He is faithful and will never let us down.

Mordecai asked the Jews near and far to celebrate annually the days when the Jews were delivered from their enemies. It says in Esther 9:22 that he asked them to "observe the days as days of feasting and joy and giving presents of food to one another and gifts to the poor."

In the musical, *Luv Esther*, we decided to finish the show with this theme of celebration, giving and salvation. We felt that the celebration theme and in particular the giving to the poor was a suitable climax and inspiration for action in today's world as the next chapter explains.

Breaking in at the end of the song is a huge thunder crash and Mordecai's words appear on the screen as a reminder to us all:

> **"Who knows . . . maybe you have come to the kingdom for such a time as this."**

Bible Study Notes

Read Esther 8:14 – 10:3.

1. Read Romans 8:31. Write down what this tells you about our God. Spend time thanking Him for who He is.

2. Mordecai instructs the Jews to remember what God has done by celebrating annually. Think through/discuss and write down why this was important.

3. Look at the way the Jews were instructed to celebrate. See Esther 9:20–22 and write down/discuss what you can learn through this.

4. Memorise Romans 15:13 and apply this verse to each difficult circumstance you face in life.

Epilogue

Many other nations still at risk.

The story of *Luv Esther* now transports us to the twenty-first century. Up on the screen come the words:

During this performance of *Luv Esther* over 800 people have died from the effects of AIDS.

This show is dedicated to one of the world's many victims.

For the Love of Juliet

As I said at the beginning of this book, the brief life of an African child, Juliet, was one of the inspirations for this musical. Juliet impacted many people's lives during her ten years and through *Luv Esther* her life once more throws out a challenge to us to reach out with love and compassion.

When Ray visited South Africa he met beautiful little Juliet. He didn't realise it at the time, but she had only two weeks to live. Her amazing story had a profound effect on his life. A number of years previously, a care worker in South Africa heard that a lady called Primrose was in great distress and deep difficulties and went to see if he could help. He visited the small shack where she lived with her two children to discover a horrific situation. Primrose was HIV positive and her daughter, Juliet, who was also living with the effects of AIDS was extremely ill. Her young son, Themba, was thankfully HIV negative. Primrose had no money or support and had run out of options. The care worker discovered that Primrose had got some rope and was on her way to the nearby railway track to tie herself and her two children to the tracks as she felt she did not have any other way out of this awful situation. The whole family was taken to Sparrow Rainbow Village, the world's first AIDS village, where they found love, compassion, support, and most of all God.

Just shortly after Ray left South Africa, Juliet called her "mothers" (her real mum and the carers who had looked after her) to her bed and said goodbye. Little Juliet's brief life was over.

A few weeks later, one of Juliet's carers, Lynette Nel, wrote an article for a magazine based on her experience of looking after this special little girl. It was from this article that Ray based the song, "For the Love of Juliet".

When Ray first read the lyrics to me, I was busy in my kitchen preparing a meal with lots of issues on my mind. However, as he read the song to me, I couldn't stop the tears pouring down my face. Allow the compassion of God to fall on you as you read the words of this song:

For the Love of Juliet

I can't pretend to understand
All the reasons why
A little girl can be denied
To live instead of die
I feel her gentle eyes on me
Just a quiet look
She's thinking back to special times
Last pages of her book.

Juliet
For the love of Juliet
Ten years you walked with tiny feet
Upon this hardened earth
Your footprints hardly left a mark
To say how much, how much you're worth

I begged and even fought with her
To eat to make her strong
We played a game that made her smile
Don't tell me she was wrong
At nine it's time for bath again
She's 14 kilograms
Pretending not to see the signs
I wash her fragile arms

Juliet
For the love of Juliet
Ten years you walked with tiny feet
Upon this hardened earth
Your footprints hardly left a mark
To say how much, how much you're worth

The world has washed its hands of her
There was no love that she could eat
The early hours I cry again
She's going to slip away, away.

She's called her "mothers" to her bed
She wants to say goodbye
O little sparrow on the ground
Now spread your wings and fly

Written by Ray Goudie/Mark Underdown/Cathy Burton/Mark Vallance
Published by Curious? Music UK/ngm/Bucks Music Ltd/MCS Music
Ltd © 2005

The biblical story of Esther is about one person making a difference in her society. Esther was a laid-down lover of God. She had the love and compassion of God pumping through her veins and because of this made a huge difference in her world. Every one of us can make a huge difference wherever God has put us. All our involvement in our society needs to come from our intimacy with Jesus.

During the epilogue, Ray is shown on video with a poignant and important message for us all and I want to share what he said here:

"There are many 'Juliets' with so many needs. This is a time of great challenge not only in Africa but in the western world too. I am asking if you will become an 'Esther' and make a difference to our world. We, like Esther can experience love, favour and deep intimacy with the King and so reach out with His compassion, not because we're told to but because we want to! I believe we have all been called for such a time as this, to be an Esther, making a difference in our communities, in our own nation and across the world. *Luv Esther* is choosing to highlight the pandemic of AIDS in Africa as only one significant way you can help. There are many other ways, especially in our own communities, right on our own doorstep.

I and some of the *Luv Esther* cast, recently visited South Africa, the home of the first AIDS village and also the place that loved and cared for Juliet. It is a shining example of what can be done in difficult and overwhelming times. I am asking you to give to projects just like this.* We are working in partnership with Christian Aid, Open Arms International, The Bible Society and with Missionary Aviation Fellowship

---

* See page 115 for details of how to give to the *Luv Esther* campaign.

**and all your money will go directly to projects that
are helping to serve local African initiatives which are
working to 'Make poverty history'."**

As Ray says, Africa is only one area which needs the love
of God, there are many others, some on our very own doorstep. God is calling for us all to be worshippers who will be
prepared to allow the love of God to soak us and drench us
and then to go out with that love pouring from our very
being and allow others to experience Jesus through us. What a
huge difference we could make if we only look into the eyes of
Jesus and allow Him to kiss us with His love. We must step
out of our comfort zones and be involved in the society we
live in; carrying His compassion to the poor, the hurting and
the lost. Do remember each of us has been called to the
Kingdom for such a time as this...

Giving to the *Luv Esther* Campaign

If you wish to give to the *Luv Esther* campaign, then please do so by sending your donation to:

> ngm
> Caedmon Complex
> Bristol Road
> Thornbury
> Bristol
> BS35 3JA
> United Kingdom

Please make your cheques payable to "Luv Esther". Every penny of your money will go to help the people on the ground working to relieve poverty and those living with HIV.

AN EXCITING CHALLENGE ALL FOR THE LOVE OF JULIET

What could YOU do with a free DVD?

We are producing a DVD entitled 'For The Love Of Juliet' which includes footage from our recent trip to Africa and the song as seen in the show. This is the challenge: We will give you one copy per family absolutely free for you to show to your youth group, church, family or friends to raise finance to help support those living in poverty and living with HIV. Use your imagination and creativity to see how much money you can raise through this DVD eg. if 10,000 people raise £10 each, that would be £100,000!

To order you copy, please contact the ngm office (01454 414880) or email info@luvesther.com

Luv Esther, luv justice!

Luv Esther Partners and Supporters

Partners

The Lancaster Foundation

Christian Aid – www.christian-aid.org.uk

Bible Society – www.biblesociety.org.uk

MAF (Missionary Aviation Society) – www.maf-uk.org

Open Arms International – www.openarmsinternational.com

Premier Christian Radio – www.premier.org.uk

Supporters

UCB – www.ucb.co.uk

Alove – www.salvationarmy.org.uk/alove

Wigwam – www.wigwam,co.uk

Soul Survivor – www.soulsurvivor.co.uk

Fierce – www.fiercedistribution.com

Oasis – www.oasistrust.org

The Message – www.message.org.uk

Care Trust – www.care.org.uk

REMEMBER YOU HAVE

BEEN CALLED FOR SUCH

A TIME AS THIS

For exciting opportunities
www.ngm.org.uk

ngm

Ray and Nancy are the directors and leaders of ngm (new generation music and mission). In 1980 God very clearly called Ray and Nancy to leave their home in Scotland and come to England to work as missionaries in the youth culture. During their first nine months of Christian work they founded and birthed in prayer the band/team ministry they called Heartbeat. Nancy was one of the singers and Ray was the drummer. Through the work of Heartbeat they literally saw thousands come to know God for themselves.

In 1985, God gave them a deep desire in their hearts for revival and a strong conviction that a new outpouring of His Spirit was going to take place in the nations of the world. During this time they also brought this prophetic message to millions of people as they released singles that broke into the mainstream charts. Heartbeat appeared on many radio and television shows including the BBC's chart programme *Top of the Pops*. As their ministry continued to develop and in line with their growing vision to see a new generation reached for God, they changed their name in 1989 to ngm. With Heartbeat finishing in 1991 a new chapter had begun, with God promising even greater blessing as they continued to bring the good news to this needy and hurting generation.

They now have around 100 full-time people working with them in evangelism, music, mission and training and have seen thousands of people in Britain and abroad come into a vibrant, living relationship with the Lord Jesus. Both individually and corporately they live by faith and have seen God provide for their ministry in miraculous ways over and over again. In 2001 they completed a huge walk of faith, having seen God release three million pounds to purchase and build an amazing Missions and Arts Centre in Thornbury, Bristol, England where they are based.

They train people from the age of seventeen in evangelism, communication and their art form, whether it be singing, dancing, dj-ing, playing an instrument or worship leading. If you are interested in hearing how you can affect the youth culture of today, be trained in your art form and learn how to live by faith, then contact ngm at:

ngm
Caedmon Complex
Bristol Road
Thornbury
Bristol BS35 3JA

If you want to receive more information about the many aspects of ngm or receive our regular newsletters, then contact us at the aforementioned address. Alternatively, email us at:

ngm@ngm.org.uk

or visit our website at:

www.ngm.org.uk

Nancy Goudie's
Spiritual Health Weekends

Three Exciting Days to Transform Your Walk with God!

Would you like to be pampered physically and toned up spiritually? Nancy Goudie's Spiritual Health Weekends could be just the thing you are looking for!

Nancy Goudie runs a weekend conference at the beginning of February each year at a luxury four-star Marriot Hotel in Bristol. The weekend is for ladies of all ages. Come and enjoy the excellent food and leisure facilities (spa, steam room, sauna, fitness room and luxury pool) and also experience God through inspirational teaching and creative spiritual exercises from Nancy. Special guests include some of the talented ngm artists. Each conference is booked well in advance so please book early to avoid disappointment.

For more information and booking details contact Nancy Goudie at:

> ngm
> Caedmon Complex, Bristol Road
> Thornbury, Bristol BS35 3JA
>
> *Tel:* 01454 414880/2
> *Fax:* 01454 414812;
> *Email:* nancygoudie@nancygoudie.com

Or visit her website at:

> www.nancygoudie.com

Other Books and Products by Nancy Goudie

Books

Spiritual Health Workout
Kingsway Publications – £6.99

This unique book is practical, accessible and fun to use and will help you exercise your faith muscles and tone up your heart for God.

> "The depth of Nancy's faith and spirituality are the genuine products of years of walking with the Lord and seeking to serve Him – that's why I am recommending her writing to you."
>
> **Steve Chalke**, Oasis Trust

50 Creative Worship Ideas
Kingsway Publications – £8.99

This is the last book in the series from Kingsway called "50 Great Ideas". Nancy's book is packed with innovative, creative and fun ideas, which are designed to help you explore more of the presence of God and the power of the Holy Spirit in our lives and in our church meetings. Ideal for small groups or large church events.

H.O.T. Faith
Sovereign World – £7.99

If you want to find out about how ngm started or the amazing miracles that happened during their five year walk of faith to get their amazing missions and arts centre (Caedmon) then Nancy's book *H.O.T. Faith: Hearing, Obeying, Trusting* is the book for you. It is a book filled with stories of faith exploits and will encourage you to walk by faith every day in life.

"Whatever mountains you need to move, this remarkable book will build your faith and empower your prayers."

Pete Greig, 24/7 Prayer

All three books are available from any Christian bookshop or direct from ngm at:

www.ngm.org.uk

or:

www.nancygoudie.com

Bible Reading Planners – 50p

A superb way of systematically reading through the Bible in one or two years. You can purchase these from ngm or at:

www.nancygoudie.com

Cassettes and CDs

Journey to the Cross – Meditation Cassette and CD
Cassette: £2.00; CD: £9.99

A powerful CD and cassette that will take you to the foot of the cross to experience Christ's death and impact you with the amazing love of God.

A God Encounter – Meditation CD

£9.99

A unique meditative worship experience which will transport you to the very throne room of God.

Peace Like a River – Meditation CD

£9.99

If you have ever experienced stress, carried worries, fought fears or are just looking for an oasis in your busy life – then this CD is for you. This recording will take you to a place of tranquillity where peace, love and grace are yours in abundance. Use this CD daily and you will find peace like a river flowing through your soul. The meditation experience is ideal for those who are not Christians as well as those who are.

All the above music and meditation CDs and cassettes are available direct from ngm at:

> ngm
> Caedmon Complex, Bristol Road
> Thornbury, Bristol BS35 3JA
> *Telephone*: 01454 414880

or at the following websites:

> www.ngm.org.uk
> www.nancygoudie.com

Nancy Goudie Contact Details

Should you wish to contact Nancy, be on Ray and Nancy's prayer letter list or be part of their group of intercessors, then do write to Nancy at:

> ngm
> Caedmon Complex
> Bristol Road
> Thornbury
> Bristol BS35 3BA.
>
> *Tel*:   01454 414880/2
> *Fax*:   01454 414812
> *Email*: nancy@nancygoudie.com

Or visit:

> www.nancygoudie.com

We hope you enjoyed reading this New Wine book.
For details of other New Wine books
and a range of 2,000 titles from other
Word and Spirit publishers visit our website:
www.newwineministries.co.uk